WHAT EXPERTS
LEADERS ARE (
THE THREE CHALLENGES

"Nicolas has been on both sides; of hugely successful and struggling firm as an entrepreneur, and now as a coach to others. He shares some simple and practical ideas drawn from his years of experience and those that have mentored him. Through The Three Challenges, *Nicolas will guide you on how to grow and scale as an entrepreneur."*

—Verne Harnish, CEO, *Gazelles,*
author of *Scaling Up (Rockefeller Habits 2.0)*

"What makes this book so powerful is the brilliant combination of ideas and personal stories based on Nicolas' experience as a business owner and business consultant. I finished the book in one sitting and then immediately started to implement several ideas that were new to me. Highly recommend!"

—Jack Canfield, coauthor,
The Success Principles™ and the
Chicken Soup for the Soul® series

"In business and in life, you're either growing or you're dying! The Three Challenges *will help you grow personally as you grow professionally.*"

—**John Jantsch**, author of *Duct Tape Marketing* and *The Referral Engine*

"*Every successful business endeavor has a leader who understands that self-mastery is where it all starts. However, you must also give clear direction to your company's path and champion its performance as a whole.* The Three Challenges *is an outstanding guide and one of the few books that will walk you through the personal and business aspects of being an entrepreneur.*"

—**Mike Michalowicz,** author of *The Pumpkin Plan* and *Profit First*

"*Nicolas is a lifelong learner and a connector of people and ideas. In* The Three Challenges, *he will connect you with the best knowledge to give you a framework for growth in life and business.*"

—**Daniel Marcos**, CEO and cofounder of the *Gazelles Growth Institute*

WHAT ENTREPRENEURS ARE SAYING ABOUT *THE THREE CHALLENGES* AND NICOLAS HAUFF

"Nicolas never ceases to surprise me. When he sent me this book, I had never thought he would take the time to share his amazing entrepreneurial experiences in such a detailed, personal way, but yet … he did. The Three Challenges *is very valuable for any entrepreneur, whether already successful or beaten down once or twice but ready to go at it again."*

—Nils Rasmussen, CEO of *Solver, Inc.,* coauthor of *Business Dashboards* and *Financial Business Intelligence*, Los Angeles, CA

"There is a before and after for our business regarding the tools that Nicolas has helped us implement through his company. These tools have been key to successfully develop and fulfill our strategic plan."

—Mariano Arias, CEO, *Axentit*, Mexico

"Nicolas has worked with us implement a structured planning process that has helped us think beyond the day-to-day operations and build a long-term vision for our company."

—**Alfred Melnik,** CEO, *MR Soluciones*, Mexico
—**Carlos Roman,** CTO, *MR Soluciones*, Mexico

"As the CEO of a corporate training company, I've seen many organizations struggle. By openly sharing his own experience and discussing a set of simple and effective tools for personal and business growth, throughout The Three Challenges *Nicolas will help you develop a new entrepreneurial mind-set."*

—**Luis G. Aspuru,** CEO,
Asgar Corporation, Mexico

"The Three Challenges *is not only a practical and effective book that every business owner should read, it is also an extraordinary example of how an entrepreneur is capable of opening up and share his experiences in a way I have never seen before. After all, companies are led by people and Nicolas has gone further than others by sharing some very personal stories and a set of ideas that can help us improve all aspects of our business and personal lives."*

—Bernardo De La Cabada, CEO, GCG,
Mexico City, Mexico

"The Three Challenges *is revealing and extremely useful, a must read for every entrepreneur. By synthesizing his ample experience as a person, as a business owner, and as a coach, he manages to convey, in a simple yet powerful way, a set of ideas and tools that we should all take into account to increase our chances of success. I had the fortune to have Nicolas as a mentor when I was an emerging entrepreneur; with his unique style, he helped me build a wider vision in business and in life, for which I will always be grateful."*

—Viviana Vargas, CEO,
Lecto Systems, Mexico City, Mexico

"In The Three Challenges *you will find a combination of Nicolas' experiences as an entrepreneur, together with the most important concepts and tools that he has acquired during his journey in the business training world. His framework can help you improve your own business and lead you to a more successful and fulfilling life."*

—Alfredo Aboumrad-Padua,
Entrepreneur, Mexico City, Mexico

"Nicolas keeps impressing me with his generosity! The Three Challenges *is a book written from the bottom of his heart and the experiences he has gained in the diverse companies he has founded, the years of learning from the great masters, and now as a mentor and advisor. This book is a path to success which includes proven tools, not only from the perspective of the business, but also from the personal growth point of view of an entrepreneur."*

—Modesto Gutierrez, CEO,
Tu Casa Express, Mexico City, Mexico

"Nicolas is a great friend and a leader in his field and his community. He is always pushing the field of entrepreneurship forward. He is as generous a teacher as he is as inquisitive a student, and that is reflected in his work, thoughts, and in this book."

—**Isaac Lekach,** serial entrepreneur,
Miami, FL

the
THREE
CHALLENGES

—the—
THREE
CHALLENGES

How to Become the **Strategy-Based Leader**

that the **Modern Business World** Demands

NICOLAS HAUFF

Published by Advantage, Charleston, South Carolina.
Member of Advantage Media Group.

ADVANTAGE is a registered trademark and the Advantage colophon is a trademark of Advantage Media Group, Inc.

ISBN: 978-1-59932-490-6
LCCN: 2015952495

Cover design by Megan Elger.

This publication is designed to provide accurate and authoritative information in regard to the subject matter covered. It is sold with the understanding that the publisher is not engaged in rendering legal, accounting, or other professional services. If legal advice or other expert assistance is required, the services of a competent professional person should be sought.

Advantage Media Group is proud to be a part of the Tree Neutral® program. Tree Neutral offsets the number of trees consumed in the production and printing of this book by taking proactive steps such as planting trees in direct proportion to the number of trees used to print books. To learn more about Tree Neutral, please visit **www.treeneutral.com.**

Advantage Media Group is a publisher of business, self-improvement, and professional development books. We help entrepreneurs, business leaders, and professionals share their Stories, Passion, and Knowledge to help others Learn & Grow. Do you have a manuscript or book idea that you would like us to consider for publishing? Please visit **advantagefamily.com** or call **1.866.775.1696.**

To my kids, Jonathan and Nicole, the most precious human beings in my life.

To Tomas, my brother and best friend.

And to the loving memory of my parents.

ABOUT THE AUTHOR

Nicolas Hauff brings more than 25 years of experience as an entrepreneur and advisor in the areas of information technology and business training.

Born and raised in Mexico City from a German father and a British-Austrian mother, he has a multinational background, is fully trilingual, and has traveled extensively for business, education, and pleasure.

Having been through successes and struggles in his own entrepreneurial path, Nicolas has a huge passion for candidly sharing his knowledge and experiences with other business owners to help them avoid the most common pitfalls and thrive as entrepreneurs. For this purpose he has established partnerships with some of the most respected international thought leaders and their organizations, having provided hundreds of entrepreneurs in Mexico and Latin America with the necessary tools for growth in their personal and business lives.

He is a proud and actively involved member of the world renowned Entrepreneur's Organization and a certified coach by Gazelles International, a worldwide association of independent executive business coaches focusing primarily on the development of mid-sized companies.

He is also a cofounder and shareholder of Krezko, a training and coaching firm for small businesses, that remotely delivers the well-known EMyth, Pumpkin Plan, and Profit First programs in Spanish.

Nicolas is an avid learner; he enjoys reading, connecting with people, traveling, and regularly attending international workshops and conferences.

On a personal basis and through his firm, he offers keynote speaking, seminars, workshops, and coaching.

To find out more, please visit www.TheThree-Challenges.com.

FOREWORD

"The stress drove me to lock myself in the private bathroom I had in my office back then and start to cry."

Thus began the author's journey of self-discovery, which has lead to this book you are about to read. How did he get there? How do we get there—to a place where we feel so out of control, not knowing what to do next? How do we find our way out?

Read on.

The author, Nicolas Hauff, and I met in the fall of 2012 at a business growth conference, and I noticed there was something unique about him. His countenance and outlook seemed "authentically bright," beyond much of what I had experienced before in the many people I've met through time, travel, and career. Over the past three years since our first meeting, in observing Nicolas, I have become convinced that what I see is who he really is. I find this both fascinating and appealing. And when Nicolas asked me to contribute to his book, *The Three Challenges*, I was as much honored as I was humbled by his request. For me, this book is the gift of his journey toward greater self-awareness and personal growth, given to all of us, to help you and I on our own journeys toward success.

As this beautiful story unfolds, Nicolas offers practical principles and tools to help you complete your journey and perhaps to help someone else in their journey too.

AN EQUATION FOR SUCCESS— THE PATH TO SUCCESS

Let's begin with the end in mind, as the great teacher Dr. Stephen Covey would encourage us to do. We all wish to live a successful life—you wouldn't be reading this book if you didn't—but how do we do so?

In this book, Nicolas puts forth an important equation for a successful life for us to reflect on:

Personal Purpose + Self-Awareness + Learning
(leads to)
a Successful Life

And as you will find as you read on, Nicolas' story illustrates the truth of this equation. He gives us key "how to's" to help that narrative become personal, practical, and actionable for you and I in our journeys.

How does one put this equation into motion in our lives? With pragmatism, Nicolas addresses the path to a successful life, based on his own pain and discovery, in three important, sequential challenges:

"Mastering yourself first" rightly focuses on the most important, and difficult, entity to gain mastery over on the road to a successful life: you. In this section, Nicolas provides a simple and practical process (with tools) to help you move in the direction of self-mastery. It can be a laborious and, at times, discouraging process, but take heart: Greatness awaits on the other side of this discovery process (which, to be honest, never really ends!).

"Mastering (your company's) direction" comes next, but growth company CEOs often place it first in life. How do we know this? Have you observed the number of CEOs with broken marriages, addictions, and mental imbalances? Self-mastery is paramount. Only then are you ready to master the direction of your company through a relevant, aligned shared vision and set of core values. Nicolas offers insights into how he did this and how to keep your company's direction current as times, economies, and technologies change.

"Mastering (your company's) performance" is the third step to success and requires an ongoing balance between "results orientation" and "relationship building." It requires paying equal attention and investing in both "cash" and "culture" in your company. In this section, Nicolas provides guidance on practical tools to achieve and maintain this dynamic balance.

Finally, one of the most important phrases in the entire book is in lesson three (found in chapter 2): "It is all about the stories that you tell yourself." It is the unseen narrative that plays out in the seven inches between your two ears that will ultimately dictate your direction and success in life. What stories are you telling yourself? Do you wish to change them?

Read on.

—Keith Brian Cupp

CEO, *Gazelles International Coaching Association*

TABLE OF CONTENTS

About the Author...*xv*

Foreword..*xvii*

INTRODUCTION: 1
A Model for Growth and Fulfillment *1*

SECTION ONE: 11
New Awareness

A Simple Question... *11*

The Pursuit of Purpose *19*

SECTION TWO: 35
Twelve Lessons for Life and Business

Lesson 1:

Nothing Lasts Forever *38*

Lesson 2:

Setbacks and Problems Can Become Sources of Growth *40*

Lesson 3:

It Is All About the Stories That You Tell Yourself.. *44*

Lesson 4:
Find Flow to Be Happier.................................. 47

Lesson 5:
Dare to Put a Shark in Your tank 49

Lesson 6:
Eating a Frog a Day Is Healthy........................ 51

Lesson 7:
Asking Is Powerful 54

Lesson 8:
If You Want to Have Friends,
Start by Being One 57

Lesson 9:
Make Networking a Habit 60

Lesson 10:
Don't Fall in Love with Your First Ideas 64

Lesson 11:
Know When to Quit 66

Lesson 12:
Use SMART Goals and Rhythm 69

SECTION THREE: 73
The Three Challenges

Challenge 1:
Mastering Yourself First.................................... 77

Challenge 2:
Mastering Your Company's Direction............. 101

Challenge 3:
Mastering Your Company's Performance *138*

FINAL THOUGHTS: 171
It All Starts with You *171*

RESOURCES: 177
Recommended Reading *177*

Other Resources *182*

ACKNOWLEDGEMENTS: 183

INTRODUCTION

A MODEL FOR GROWTH AND FULFILLMENT

I have been told in many forms that I am, by my nature, a connector. Whenever I can, I will connect you with people, and I will connect you with ways to acquire new knowledge. This is my passion: to learn new things, to meet new people, and to introduce you to one another, as a way of making you aware of concepts and opportunities that you might never have considered and that can produce breakthrough results for you.

In the pages ahead, you will be introduced to a model for growth and fulfillment in life and in business. Many books have been written about life's challenges, and many have been written about business challenges. This book is about *your life in business.* It is meant for you, the entrepreneur, who besides having the huge responsibility of leading and growing your business, is also a human being with feelings, struggles, aspirations, and needs in all areas of your life.

From my own experience in business, from my ongoing interactions with many other business owners from different countries around the world, and from what I have learned in the business training and coaching profession, I have identified three core challenges that, as entrepreneurs, we all must master in order to reach greater heights:

1. We must become and remain fully aware of ourselves by understanding who we are as individuals, why we do what we do, how we add value to others, and where we want to go.

2. We must build and maintain a common vision of the direction our company is going.

3. We must take consistent action to get great performance.

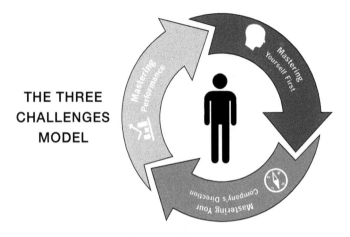

THE THREE CHALLENGES MODEL

The experiences that I relate here will be mostly my own. However, this book is not an autobiography; I am opening myself up to illustrate the concepts that I am about to discuss with stories about things that I have lived and lessons that I have learned. My intent is that you will benefit from these stories and will be able to relate them to your own circumstances. In large part, this book will focus on those three challenges and how I have come to understand them.

I will build upon this model, and in future writings I plan to relate more of the experiences that others have faced in dealing with these challenges. My goal will be to continue connecting you with the wisdom and with the tools we all need in order to grow as human beings and as entrepreneurs.

Henry Ford once said that if he lost all his fortune, he could regain it within several years. He would know how to do that because he knew what had made him successful.

I was very successful in an information technology business for years until I hit a severe setback between 2007 and 2008. As I stood in that difficult situation, I realized that I wasn't really aware of what had made me successful and why my success was suddenly slipping away. After assimilating my losses, I began a time of self-discovery to uncover both, the roots of my success and the obstacles that stood in the way.

As a completely unexpected benefit of this self-discovery process, I was introduced to a new but fascinating opportunity: the world of personal and business growth programs where I became acquainted with a wide array of concepts and tools that I wished I had known before. I also realized how many others must have been struggling in that same situation of running their companies the best they could and not being equipped with the necessary tools.

Since then, I have developed a big passion and become actively involved with these programs, part-nering with some of the leading international content and program providers and thus helping other entrepreneurs expand their awareness, grow as individuals, and grow their businesses.

Over the years, that journey is what led me to recognize the three challenges and understand how my lack of awareness of them had impacted my business and my life. I personally had not fully done whatever was necessary to grow as a leader and meet the new demands of my growing business. I had not maintained a unified vision for the company as it grew. And I had not consistently made things happen. I realized that this was where I had fallen short on each challenge.

"Perhaps you should split your information into three books," a colleague suggested to me after I consulted with him and others about this project. "You could have a separate book on each of the three challenges. After all," he said, "George Lucas decided to make several Star Wars movies because he had too much of a story for just one."

I considered his idea for a while, but that's just not the way I think. I tend to think top-down, starting at 30,000 feet and then zooming in closer. For that reason, the three challenges appear right at the start, in this book, so you can see the model upon which the ideas are organized.

So much good material is available, and my goal is to connect you with the best. Whenever you read a book, take a class, attend a conference, or enroll in a program, you gain from what many others have already learned and experienced. As an entrepreneur and as a business advisor, my teams and I make use of the wisdom provided by world-class expert organizations for business and personal growth, such as:

- Gazelles and The Rockefeller Habits, founded by Verne Harnish (strategy planning and execution for growth companies)

- E-Myth, founded by Michael E. Gerber (small business transformation)

- The Canfield Training Group, founded by Jack Canfield (human potential)

- The John Maxwell Team, founded by John Maxwell (leadership)

- Duct Tape Marketing, founded by John Jantsch (marketing strategies and tactics)

- The Pumpkin Plan/Profit First, co-created by Mike Michalowicz (growth tools for entrepreneurs)

- Strategyzer, founded by Alexander Osterwalder (business model generation)

- Life Purpose Institute, founded by Fern Gorin (life coaching)

There are also many other great sources besides the ones listed before. When people ask me whether they should go for A, B or C, I answer, "You will most likely benefit from all but in the right context of your life and business and in the right sequence." My intention is to help you find the common denominators of all that wisdom.

I offer you *The Three Challenges* as a model for personal growth as an entrepreneur. However, this is far more than just a retelling of other people's ideas. I have lived through countless experiences that have given me a unique perspective. I have seen success, experienced troubled times in my life and career, and reassessed myself. If you have known these kinds of experiences yourself, you know what I am talking about. Be assured that I empathize with you.

I have divided this book into three sections:

SECTION ONE - NEW AWARENESS

The purpose of this section is to share with you my background, my beliefs, and my experiences of finding self-awareness. My intent here is to create a connecting link with you that I hope we will keep throughout the book. I expect that this way you can better understand the context from which I drew conclusions on the challenges entrepreneurs face.

SECTION TWO - TWELVE LESSONS FOR LIFE AND BUSINESS

In this section I share 12 of the most valuable lessons I have learned during my life as an entrepreneur and as a business advisor, with the intent of laying the foundation for you to better understand and apply The Three Challenges model in your own life.

SECTION THREE - THE THREE CHALLENGES

This section explains The Three Challenges model, providing you with a set of some of the most valuable tools I have learned that will help you master each challenge and further develop your growth as an entrepreneur.

As I mentioned before, this book will act as the flagship for further material that I intend to integrate, inviting others to share their ideas, experiences, and tools. Perhaps you may be one of them. First, however, we need the right context—and these three challenges provide a basis on which to build.

You no doubt have your own specific needs and will implement your own best solutions that I will be happy to learn about. Let us embark together on this journey of discovery and vision. Let's make it happen!

SECTION ONE

NEW AWARENESS

A SIMPLE QUESTION

"Dad, can we go to the bookstore?"

I still remember these words as if it was yesterday. My two young children came to me with that request on a Saturday morning in May of 2008 in our Mexico City home—and as I reflect on that moment, I realize it was when I embarked on a journey that would change me forever.

My son, who was ten, wanted a copy of the *Guinness Book of World Records*. My daughter, who was almost four, looked forward to the picture books in the children's section. And I have long been a lover of books and all the perspectives and knowledge that they offer.

They did not have to ask twice. "Yes," I said. "We will go to the bookstore." And so I ushered them out into the bright day, closing the door behind me.

That spring was a difficult time for me, for many reasons. Personally, I was going through a period of grief and a paralyzing feeling of guilt in a way I had never experienced before. If one is to move forward in life, such a destructive feeling of guilt cannot continue; it must be overcome.

And times were tough, as well, at my information technology business. Though I had seen plenty of success from 2001 through 2006, a variety of factors were changing that good fortune.

The economic crisis that had started in late 2007 was heating up, and we were feeling the volatility in the stock market and the housing crisis. Something strange had been in the air for many months. Oil prices were going up, with predictions of $200 per barrel. There was talk of food scarcity. People could see the big recession taking shape.

At our company, we were feeling stressed. We were struggling and losing money. Although we were still growing and generating a lot of revenue, many of our projects were unprofitable, and our overhead expenses were way too large. We had grown too fast and become disorganized—going in too many directions. **The operations of my business had clearly outgrown me**, and I didn't have a clue on how to turn the situation around. I was in a state of drifting—downhill.

It was tough. I remember one day getting a series of complaints both from employees and from customers—four complaint calls in a row. My accountant also dropped by to let me know that we were at risk of not making payroll the following week. The stress drove me to lock myself in the private bathroom I had in my office back then and start to cry.

AN AWAKENING AMID STRESS

As the months went by and things got worse, both in business and in life, I was sinking into worry, stress, and depression, and those feelings were deepening each day. Such was my state when my children asked to go to the bookstore that Saturday morning.

Sometimes, it is the hard things we go through that equip us to become stronger. I did not know it then, but I know it today, and I am far more self-aware than I was several years ago.

At my company, for example, I can see now that I was responsible for much of what happened. I did not react soon enough to the economic crisis. I did not pursue the professional advice that I needed to reduce costs and put the business back in order.

And if I were to pinpoint when my journey of self-awareness began, I would say it was on that day when my children asked me to take them to the bookstore, just a couple of blocks from our home. I am a reader, and I am no stranger to bookstores. Whenever I visit the United States, I enjoy a trip to Barnes & Noble, one of my favorite stores because of the experience it offers. At the time, however, I had not read books in a long while. Sometimes I would buy books and just shelve them.

But on that day, something life changing happened.

As my children were occupied, I was going through the aisle of self-help books. I scanned the titles and saw Robert Kiyosaki's *Rich Dad Poor Dad*. I thought, "Oh, I already have that one." It was among the volumes sitting unread on my bookshelf.

Then I noticed several books by Carlos Cuauh-témoc Sanchez, a Mexican best-selling author and speaker. One of them was *I Dare You to Prosper*. When I opened it, I saw that the first chapter was titled "Audit Your Crisis." I thought about my own life, and I resolved that I would buy that book and read it cover to cover. Why this book? I wanted to read *I Dare You to Prosper* because I was having financial and business problems.

THE BEGINNING OF MY JOURNEY OF SELF-DISCOVERY

Thus began my journey of self-discovery. I scheduled a weekend away from the city by myself to read and think. I also had been seeing a counselor who suggested that such a weekend would be a good step.

I decided not to go anywhere familiar. I wasn't going to go to Puerto Vallarta, to Los Cabos, or to Cancun, which held memories and potential distractions for me. Nor did I need a fancy hotel. I love the beaches and beautiful coasts of Mexico, so I went to La Paz in Baja California. I took my computer with me to start writing.

And so I went to the beach with my book, a pencil, and some paper for a time of introspection. I wrote a lot about myself and my feelings, and I also scribbled in the margins of the book as inspirations came to me. In the evening, I ordered room service and transferred my notes into my computer.

In doing so, I found one of the best self-awareness tool that I have ever known—and that is to read a book on a topic that is relevant for you, underline or highlight passages that draw your attention, and take plenty of notes relating it to your life. It's a powerful path to inspiration.

I Dare You to Prosper opens with an exploration of where one's crisis originates. It looks at money and prosperity not only from a financial point of view but also from a personal growth point of view.

The journey that began that day in the bookstore has not ended. It was the first step of my awakening to who I really am. It was the beginning of a quest that would breathe new energy not only into my business but also into my life.

Those words, "I dare you to prosper," were what I needed to hear—and the book contains a great message for all of us in these times. When I came back from La Paz, I went to my bookshelf and pulled out *Rich Dad, Poor Dad*, one of the works that Sanchez references in *I Dare You to Prosper*. I had purchased the popular Kiyosaki book in 2002 or 2003, when my career was thriving. I did little more than thumb through it back then; I remember thinking, in my arrogance, that I didn't need it. I felt that I already was doing most of what Kiyosaki was explaining. I was wrong. This time, I read *Rich Dad, Poor Dad* and *The Cash-Flow Quadrant*, both by Kiyosaki, from cover to cover. These books led me to *The E-Myth: Why Most Small Businesses Don't Work and What to Do About It* by Michael Gerber. And that book, in particular, has been a breakthrough in my life.

This process was having a big impact on me, and now I was also starting on the course to a better understanding on how to run a company and how to relate with my business stakeholders—although that atmosphere would get a lot worse before it improved. By the fall of 2008, my business life felt like a catastrophe. But at the same time, I was growing personally and awakening to possibilities. This was indeed a time of new beginnings.

Since then, I have read countless business and personal development books. I have regularly attended international courses, workshops, and conferences on related topics. I have met many thought leaders, best-selling authors, and speakers. I have been trained and mentored by leading international experts. I have had the opportunity to interact on a regular basis with other entrepreneurs to share our experiences, not only on business topics but also on personal and family topics.

As we seek knowledge, it comes to us through a variety of avenues. It is said that the teacher is there whenever the student is ready. When we are eager to learn and to grow, we do. One resource lays the groundwork for others, and that is what I want to offer you in the chapters to come.

THE PURSUIT OF PURPOSE

I first got connected with my life purpose in January of 2009. It was a very difficult time, and I was feeling sorry for myself. "Why am I in this situation?" I wondered, "Why are other people I've mentored doing so much better than me right now?"

At the time I was reading a variety of inspirational and self-development books and keeping a journal of my thoughts. One was Napoleon Hill's classic work, *Think and Grow Rich*, which has a chapter called "Definiteness of Purpose." After a while, I put the book aside and started writing what I believed my own life purpose to be.

After writing up several pages, this is what I came up with: "I am constantly learning new things and meeting new people. I connect people with people, and people with knowledge. I feel fulfilled when a connection that I make for someone brings that person great results."

Why had others excelled after I had mentored them? Because I had put them in the right place. I had effectively connected them. I helped them to find the right things at the right time.

That's my life's purpose, I realized—and what I needed to do was to figure out how to build upon it so that I could make a living from it. And I knew that "a living" meant more than money. I needed to organize my life around that purpose in everything I did.

SUCCESS FOLLOWS PURPOSE AND SELF-AWARENESS

Each of us has a purpose. I believe that everybody and everything in the universe have a reason for being, and early in life we should develop an awareness of it. Don't wait until you are middle-aged to discover your own purpose.

The lesson for the entrepreneur is clear: if you want to build a successful and fulfilling business, the way to do that is to first lead a fulfilling life. In other words; find your purpose, become more self aware, and then your success is most likely to follow.

When I went into business in 1996, I still had a lot to discover about myself. I believe that many of us spend years of our lives unaware of who we are, why we are here, and where we are going. When we live that way, our lives become aimless as we just go with the flow, accepting whatever happens.

Many people end up just doing things to please others. They do what others want—or what they think others want. Some spend a lifetime trying to please their parents or other stakeholders in their lives. They are trying to live according to the "establishment."

Or they simply need to make a living, and they see no way out of their position. They may believe they are doing the proper thing, but they never come to know themselves. It is as if they live under a gray cloud. All the landscape will be gray. If they try their hand at a business, it will lack the color of their passions and, most likely, of their strengths.

Such patterns start early in life. Our educational system can actually thwart the development of our self-awareness. It can be quite rigid—or at least that seemed to be the case for me, thirty-some years ago. My parents wanted the best for me, I'm sure, but I had a hard time in school. By today's standards, perhaps I would have been diagnosed with ADHD—but in several occasions, I have been able to use it to my advantage because of the creativity and big picture vision accompanying it.

What I may have needed in school was more attention to my creative side. I'm a dreamer, an idea person, and I have learned that I do best when I team up with people who work together with me at executing these ideas.

I help connect people who need to be together to make the most of their individual abilities and talents. I find it fulfilling when I can connect people in business, but I also get deep satisfaction from simply recommending a book that helps somebody.

In large part, that is why I wrote this book. I love to learn, and by sharing my story with as many people as possible, my hope is that I can influence their lives for the better. I want to help you tap into what is extraordinary within you.

BECOMING AWARE OF YOUR REAL DRIVER FOR SUCCESS

Many times, what makes you successful in something is not necessarily what you think it is. There may be other drivers behind your success that you may not even be aware of. It is important that you find what those drivers are so you can recognize a pattern and do more of it.

In my case, I started my career as an IT consultant and sold software solutions before opening my own consulting business. After I started my own business, I was successful for many years—but I realize now that it wasn't necessarily because I was a great IT professional. I was successful because I'm a great connector. As mentioned before, that is my fundamental skill and purpose in life, and I had chosen IT as the platform to express it, even though I was unaware of this strength and how to consciously make use of it until my early 40s. By launching and building my own IT consulting business, I was putting my natural inclinations to good use. I was connecting with people.

I got into an industry in a rapid growth mode, and I was able to apply my connector skills so that I managed to grow a sizeable business because I was able to put the right things and the right people in place at the right time.

And this has been the hardest but most valuable lesson to learn in my business life. In truth, I was unaware of the root of my successes up until I entered my crisis in 2008. And I had been very successful: my company grew year after year and received the Microsoft Dynamics award as the best Latin American partner of the year for four years in a row. In 2006, at my peak, we were presented four international awards from Microsoft, which at that time was quite unusual for a single partner to get.

I received much professional recognition, and my business was thriving. I did not understand, however, that deep inside, my passion and strengths were lying somewhere else. Had I realized that, I would have reinvented myself sooner. I would have gotten professional help to redesign the governance of my business without necessarily leaving it, and things may have been different. But business was good then, and there was a big component of "ego" on my side. I wasn't willing to let go of my leadership position. It wasn't until a few years later, when I was in the mud, that I began my journey of change.

In the early 2000s, I had a business partner who was certainly a more focused manager than I was. When our business was structured in such a way that we complemented each other, we accomplished great things. But there came a time when we structured the business in a way that each of us was running a separate unit within our group. We started competing instead of collaborating—and I was falling behind in performance.

"What you do best," he had told me at one point, "is forming relationships between people." But I didn't take that piece of wisdom to heart at that time.

It was not until years after we split that I came to understand what had made our partnership succeed at the beginning and what had made it fail in the end. I have also come to the conclusion that one can reinvent oneself without abandoning a lifetime of work. You don't have to change careers, but you can change how you relate to your career.

TAKING A NEW PATH

After I had gone through that period of struggle, I decided by mid 2009 that I needed to step aside and bring somebody else to run the company, so I invited a friend of mine to join as a business partner and CEO. He had spent his past six years in the corporate world, and I considered that he had better management skills than me.

We planned a six-month transition time and, as he completely took over the operation in 2010, I started to think more seriously about becoming a business coach as a way of having a framework that would help me share all my experiences inside and outside my own businesses. Released from my day-to-day responsibilities, I could pursue my passion this way.

Following that idea and after exploring different options, I became a Gazelles International Coach in 2012, and today I serve my own companies as well as select personal clients using the *Four Decisions*^{TM} methodology. I am also one of the founders, together with Pablo Hernandez O'Hagan, Rodrigo Laddaga, and three other entrepreneurs, of a company called Krezko that does training and coaching for small businesses in Mexico. Through that company, established in 2008, we deliver the renowned *E-Myth*, *Pumpkin Plan,* and *Profit First* programs in Spanish and plan to release additional ones in the future.

Under the leadership of Rodrigo at Krezko, we have been implementing a scalable system to deliver these programs remotely. We have worked hard to achieve a great reputation. We have been featured in *Entrepreneur Magazine* and other publications in Mexico, and our system has also allowed us to serve clients in other Latin American countries and even in Africa. (Yes, there is a small country in Africa called Equatorial Guinea where Spanish is one of the official languages).

APPLYING NEW SKILLS IN BUSINESS

In *The E-Myth* book, Michael Gerber describes three personalities of a business owner: the *entrepreneur*, the *manager*, and the *technician*. After I stepped aside and allowed our new CEO to lead, I thought that I was not going to be a manager anymore. I was going to take the role of the entrepreneur who finds opportunities, develops ideas, and puts things together.

However, what I have learned over the years is that no matter what role you take in your company, you still need to acquire and apply the discipline and the skills of a manager in order to grow as an entrepreneur and be more effective in whatever endeavor you embark on.

It was precisely by applying the discipline and various skills of a manager, which our new CEO brought to the table, that we were able to turn our company around by 2010, having a few good years thereafter.

However, by 2013 we experienced problems again; this time caused by a combination of adverse market conditions, two bad hires in our leadership team, and the effect of not having paid enough attention earlier on to the product direction of one of our strategic partners.

Business conditions are changing at a higher pace every day, so you cannot afford to rest on your laurels and think that past successes will guarantee your success in the future.

By mid 2014, our CEO left the company to pursue other projects. I took back the leadership and appointed an existing director to help me oversee the day-to-day operations. We chose to divide the company into smaller business units and closely monitor each one of them in order to decide which ones we were going to focus on and which ones we were going to let go of.

By acquiring personal and business coaching skills, I can now serve my own businesses in a better way. I also find that customers and other stakeholders (current and prospective) see me today as a much more interesting person, and that has helped bring in business as well. Lately, we have been working on a new vision for our company that the tools I have learned and the experience I have gathered are helping to define and advance.

As a way to turn into a better leader in your company, I strongly recommend that you acquire coaching skills and become a practitioner of business tools, such as the ones we are going to discuss in section 3.

PREVENTIVE MEDICINE

Originally, I conceived this as a book to help people who feel stuck in their business—or in life itself. By telling my own story and solutions that I found, I hoped to help others get in touch with their true talents and passions and thereby to find a better path to success.

I wanted to reach out to entrepreneurs who were feeling that they lacked a direction or sense of purpose. I am often invited to speak to students and others about that very thing, and I have found that I have a passion for doing it. I share with them my own story, and I also share the tools that I have found to be helpful on one's journey of awareness.

I tell them, however, that they must not wait to start their journey of self-awareness in the midst of a crisis at the "tender" age of 44, which is what I did. Most people do experience a crisis at some point, but it doesn't need to hit you that hard. If you use these tools, you can take the right path in your life.

In that way, this book is not just for people who are stuck in life. This is more than a cure; it is also preventive medicine. You can ease your way by anticipating where troubles are likely to arise and doing something about it in advance by investing in your personal growth and not allowing your business or your life to outgrow you.

THE IMPORTANCE OF PURPOSE FOR BUSINESS AND LIFE

Our lives as entrepreneurs go way deeper than merely business. It's important for all of us to identify what we do well and to concede what we don't do well. On my own journey, I have discovered how to contribute in more suitable ways to my company and to other organizations.

I identified my purpose and am hoping through my example and through this book to drive home the following point: **you need to be aware of why you are here, or nothing will come of it.** If you are not aware of why you are doing something, how can your efforts succeed?

This is no simple thing, but you need to do it. Even though I can share my own experiences and the tools that have helped me on my journey, each of us is a unique, complicated, and multifaceted human being. We have our relationships with our colleagues in the workplace, and we have our personal lives outside of the workplace. We have our families. We have our friendships. And you can't separate them. You can identify the elements, but you have to understand that those parts interrelate. What's going on in one area of your life is going to influence what's happening in another.

I had lunch with some fellow entrepreneurs, and we talked about life purpose. We discussed whether one discovers their life purpose or whether one defines it. Some of my colleagues maintained that we define our purpose at a point in our lives, but some of us were not convinced of that. You can define a life mission, but that is not your life purpose or your reason for being here. Rather, your life purpose is something you discover. You don't control it; you simply become aware of it in time. Then you apply it and give yourself a mission. However, that mission can change, creating different missions in pursuit of your purpose.

We had a good debate—and concluded that both views have merit. Yes, you may define your life purpose, but in that case you don't define it in this material world. We may define it or it may be defined for us in another dimension before we come to this earth. I believe that there is such a spiritual world.

We then talked a lot about the *Conversations with God* series of books at that luncheon. Another of our conclusions was that we can learn the best elements of spirituality from a variety of religions. Each has unique perspectives and we must be respectful of all of them. They are all interpretations of the universe, and I believe that we would do well by learning about them all.

In my coaching and in my keynotes, I try to draw from many sources. I look for beauty and for useful messages to bring back to people—to connect them with those concepts. We will go deeper on how you can identify your own life purpose and mission in section three when we review the first of the three challenges: *Mastering Yourself First*.

Once you gain clarity about your purpose, why you are here, and what you are good at, you can take these insights back to your business and also to your family and friends. Those insights can keep you healthy, as they will help you connect with all areas of your life.

SECTION TWO

TWELVE LESSONS FOR LIFE AND BUSINESS

My friend must have sensed, just by looking at me, how much I needed to talk to somebody. "Why don't you join our board of directors?" he asked me. "I think we need you, and you certainly need us."

This so-called board of directors was a peer group of Mexican businessmen who had been getting together regularly once a month for several years. "We can share experiences," said my friend, whom I had met at a software implementation project for the company he represented—a retail chain of about 80 stores.

This was in 2008—which was not, as I have explained, my best of times. I was in my early 40s at the time, and the other businessmen were in their late 50s and early 60s. We were clearly in different stages of life. They said I was bringing energy and new ideas to them, and they were bringing experience to me. They told me later that before accepting me into the group, they had joked and even placed bets on the fact that I wouldn't stand being with them for more than three months. Six years later, I was still in. Unfortunately, the group fell apart when our leader passed away in the spring of 2014.

It is critical to become involved with a group such as that, where you can just be yourself and put your issues, opportunities, and ideas on the table and openly discuss them with others. That's how it is also with EO (Entrepreneur's Organization), which I also joined in 2008, an international peer-to-peer network for entrepreneurs with thousands of members worldwide where chapters are divided into *forums,* which are groups of five to seven persons where we openly discuss business, personal, and family situations under a gestalt protocol and strict code of confidentiality. The feedback is priceless, and in sharing lessons and perspectives, we grow together.

Over the years, I have learned many things through my own experiences, from hearing the experiences of others, and through the many materials that I have studied. And I want to share with you what I've come to learn in the form of **12 primary lessons for life and for business**.

As you will see, many of the lessons in this chapter are intertwined. They relate to one another in a variety of ways, which underscores how fundamental they are to growth and fulfillment.

LESSON 1

NOTHING LASTS FOREVER

One of the most difficult things that I have learned to recognize is that **nothing lasts forever**. The only constant in this life is change.

I read a quote in a book by Mexican best-selling author Gaby Vargas that says: "When you think that you are going to live forever, it is when you do stupid things." That happened to me when I was at the peak of my career in my technology business. It's very easy to remain in your comfort zone, thinking that nothing is going to change.

But in truth, everything wears off, goes out of style, dies, or changes in time, and it is in the period of transition that crises arise. In those periods of transition, there is indeed great risk. But it is also in those periods where we find the most opportunities—when we are leaving the old behind as we enter a new stage.

The most important thing here is not to wait until a crisis arises but to remain aware of the fact that **nothing lasts forever** and develop the ability to prepare for the changes over time. From the business point of view, we will discuss the way you can develop this ability when we review the third of the three challenges: *Mastering Performance (4. Conducting a SWOT and a SWT Analysis)*.

For now, think of your own life and business and ask yourself the following questions:

- Are you sitting in your comfort zone?

- Are there any cycles coming to an end soon?

- What are the trends in your environment that could have an impact in you?

- Which potential changes make you really feel uncomfortable?

- What opportunities can you see in these potential changes?

LESSON 2

SETBACKS AND PROBLEMS CAN BECOME SOURCES OF GROWTH

My father was a consultant whose clients were mainly manufacturing companies. He was also a passionate writer and a contributor for different industrial publications.

One day he wrote an article called "Problems" and developed a workshop by the same name in which he delivered the message that problems, setbacks, and frustrations are sources of big opportunity. He even developed a methodology on how to discover opportunities inside problems.

Later, when I was going through my own crisis, his principle made a lot of sense to me. Unfortunately, he had passed away two years earlier, and I was not able to tell him. I saw that my setbacks had actually become an asset as I moved forward, because they were the source of growth. Otherwise I might have never recognized the opportunity that was right in front of me.

This was about the same time that I bought into E-Myth for the license in Mexico. One of the modules of that business coaching and training program is called "The Key Frustrations Process."

When I read that module, I realized that the essence of the message was the same as my father had published years earlier—in this case, that the greatest frustrations in your operation are the greatest sources of opportunity to build a system. Both processes help you find the root of your problems, frustrations, or setbacks.

You may recall the movie *The Perfect Storm*, in which the elements of nature culminated into a disaster, pummeling a sword-fishing boat off the coast of Massachusetts. A couple of years ago, I attended an SAP conference where the discussion turned to the "technological perfect storm," referring to the challenges that the technology trends were imposing on our industry and the way they were addressing them as a company. As with many crises, there is usually more than one cause.

At times, setbacks seem to conspire to make matters worse. It actually can be dangerous to think that the cause was only one thing. We must beware of the forces that create a perfect storm. If you really want to learn from a problem, you need to delve into the root source that generated it. Then you can have control over the storm's path and where it leads. You can turn that storm to your advantage rather than let it slam you down so that it can become a positive force in your life.

When I was thriving, I was in my own little world—my little bubble, if you will. Our group had been one of the top resellers for two of the main software companies in the world, and we had also become the largest reseller in Latin America for both companies.

It was after the big setback that I started discovering that there was a bigger world. Sure, I had been traveling a lot, and I was very well known in my industry. I had met many people, but I had yet to discover a whole new world of purpose—of how to develop one's business and oneself.

That's when I began reading intently, going to workshops, partnering with E-Myth, joining EO, and meeting with the board of directors. I met a lot of new people. Most of all, I learned a lot about myself.

The E-Myth and similar books had led me to an "aha" moment in my life that I have been eager to share with all. "Where was this book hidden ten years ago?" I asked myself when I first read *The E-Myth*.

Some years after we launched E-Myth in Mexico and had some success stories to tell about our local clients, I called up my friend, Alonso Castellot, who conducts a daily radio program for small business owners in Mexico. He had interviewed me about my software consulting company and our solutions several times. Now, years later, he was interviewing me about business coaching. The first question he asked me was, "I know you from the world of business software. Tell me, why this new venture?"

I said, "Because I realized that many entrepreneurs like myself struggle to survive, to do things better, and to thrive. I have made this a mission for me, to help other entrepreneurs struggle less and have a better life by providing them with tools, by sharing experiences with them, and by helping them expand their awareness."

Had I not had the setback that made me sensitive to life, I wouldn't have been inclined as much to search inside myself to discover my true life purpose—which is to connect people with one another and with ideas and knowledge. That has become my mission, and that setback became an asset for my new mission.

Think of your own setbacks and problems:

- What have you learned from them?

- Have you been able to see opportunities in them?

- Are you able to observe any repeating patterns?

LESSON 3

IT IS ALL ABOUT THE STORIES THAT YOU TELL YOURSELF

When I was looking at everything in a negative way, my counselor told me, "Nicolas, in the end, it is about the story you tell yourself. What story do you want to tell yourself?"

I acknowledged what she had said, but I didn't quite know what to make of it. That concept popped up again one day in 2009. I was in a car with a friend who lives in Puerto Vallarta where I visit often for business and leisure. We had gone to dinner, and he was listening to the song "Wonderwall" by Oasis. His playlist had at least five versions of that same song. Some of the versions had a lot of rhythm, and another felt nostalgic, and another version was more sensual. It was the same song with different interpretations. You can slow it down or speed it up, and the emotions change with the tempo, though the lyrics never change. This is the same in life—there are so many ways to look at a situation.

Two years later, I was invited to speak in front of 300 entrepreneurial students. As a shareholder of the licensee of E-Myth in Mexico, I was very active in our entrepreneurial community, and I felt flattered to be invited. Just the process of preparing that keynote was a breakthrough, one of many in this new era of my life. But since most of the students didn't have a business yet, the E-Myth didn't seem a suitable topic. The program is meant for practicing entrepreneurs who already are facing the struggles of a growing business.

So what would I tell these students who were only aspiring entrepreneurs? I decided I should go deeper into life lessons, deeper into what they are ought to experience. And so, I wrote a keynote called "Creating a Venture Based on Your Life Purpose," which laid the groundwork for this book. I'll always be grateful to the person who invited me to deliver that first keynote. Since then, I have been able to deliver more keynotes at different venues.

In my speeches, I play some versions of "Wonderwall," using them to illustrate the concept of "the stories that you tell yourself," and then I quote Gabriel Garcia Marquez, the prominent Colombian author who wrote *One Hundred Years of Solitude*, which is known worldwide. He said, "Life is not the one you lived but the one you remember and how you remember it to talk about it."

If you feel good, you are going to tell better stories to yourself. If you feel depressed, do something about it, and do it fast. Get professional help, and get out of that vicious cycle. And make sure you get a good night's sleep. I have discovered that when I don't, I tend to interpret things negatively the next day.

It's all tied together. If you tell yourself bad stories, you'll feel further deflated. You may not sleep as well, and you may end up telling yourself even worse stories. If you tell yourself good stories, it goes the other way, turning the situation around and upward.

LESSON 4

FIND FLOW TO BE HAPPIER

In one of the keynotes of a John Maxwell Team (JMT) conference in Orlando, Ed DeCosta, who is the JMT faculty member responsible for the sales and marketing curriculum, stated something that has stuck with me since then. He said in a very pragmatic way, just as good sales guys are: "Find your sources of happiness, happy sales persons sell more than unhappy ones."

At one point between 2003 and 2006, I was feeling frustrated. My business was going well, I was healthy, I had family and friends—and yet I was not fully happy. I was missing something. One of my friends told me, "You are not passionate about anything. You need a hobby."

In his book, *Flow: The Psychology of Happiness*, psychologist Mihaly Csíkszentmihályi says people are happiest when they are in a state of "flow"—that is, when they get so absorbed in an activity or situation that nothing else seems to matter.

After my big 2008 crisis, I began reading personal growth and development books searching for answers, and in it I also found my passion. I find "flow" in my readings, my coaching programs, my speaking engagements, the workshops that I deliver, and all the conferences that I attend. I also find it when I am preparing my workshops and keynotes.

EO, has a program called "Accelerator" that helps emerging entrepreneurs reach the one million dollars a year revenue level. As EO members, we coach and teach them on a pro-bono basis about strategy, finance, marketing, and human resources. While planning a beach vacation in Puerto Vallarta, I was also asked to conduct a workshop with EO Accelerator that same week, and so I ended up flying from Puerto Vallarta to Mexico City and back the same day just for the opportunity to be involved. It wasn't something I was paid to do; this was volunteer work.

Most of us know that feeling of falling in love. It's a similar feeling when you find your passion in life. You feel giddy. You feel content and eager to wake up and get going with your day, every day. Different people find *flow* with different things, but unless you are passionate about what you are doing, all of your efforts are likely to be just average or mediocre. They won't rise to greatness until your whole heart and soul is into what you do.

LESSON 5

DARE TO PUT A SHARK IN YOUR TANK

Japanese fishermen faced a dilemma as they ventured increasingly farther out to sea in search of a good catch. Because it took longer to get back to port, they began putting the fish in freezers aboard their boats. However, people could taste the difference, and the frozen fish fetched a lower price. The fishermen then turned to stuffing the fish into tanks. The fish were alive but simply existing. They were listless and far from delicious.

The industry finally hit on the solution. The fishermen put small sharks in the tanks, which presented the fish with quite a challenge. As they darted about to avoid those jaws, their flesh regained its texture and taste. Sure, the shark would eat some, but those that remained commanded a premium price.

The lesson is this: allow yourself to be challenged, either personally or in your company.

When I had our new partner join the company at the end of 2009, he challenged all of us. He challenged our employees, and he challenged me to do things differently. That made many people very uncomfortable, including me at times. They were complaining about the new style, but I chose to stick to it. "That's the kind of management we need for the company right now," I told them. The new style and ideas yielded good results for the following two to three years.

When I go to my monthly EO Forum meeting, we are all surrounded by "sharks." The seven people in the group give their personal updates, and some of us get to present specific situations or projects. And then each of us is challenged by the other. When I have presented my ideas for this book to them, for example, they asked me tough but useful questions.

This is the idea of "putting a shark in your tank." Be willing to accept feedback, even if it's hard feedback. When I went through the *Rich Dad* coaching program for entrepreneurs in 2008, as one of the first activities, I took a personality test. It told me that I was bold and a visionary and that I saw opportunities where others did not. But on the negative side, it told me that I was not very open to feedback. I've been working on that. My involvement in business coaching, as well as being part of my peer groups, have helped me open up for feedback. That's the kind of benefit you get from "putting a shark in your tank."

That's what a good counselor does for you. That's also what a good coach does for you. That's what good accountability partners do for you. And that's what a good advisory board does for you and your company. They all seek your commitment, hold you accountable, ask you tough questions, and challenge you, so you keep on moving.

LESSON 6

EATING A FROG A DAY IS HEALTHY

At times, when I have found myself putting things off or unable to concentrate on my work—or not even wanting to get out of bed—I've asked myself: "Have I eaten my frog today?"

If I'm just scurrying around in the morning doing busy work, I know I need to gulp down that frog. Sometimes, I write down its name on a Post-It—a green one, like a frog—and then I grab it by the legs and open wide.

It's not a tasty meal. But I do know this: anything else I eat that day will taste far better.

Eat That Frog! is the name of a book by Brian Tracy, who recommends that very thing. The book's subtitle is: "21 Great Ways to Stop Procrastinating and Get More Done in Less Time." His point is to identify your most difficult task each day and to tackle it right away. If you eat one frog each morning, it's the worst thing that's going to happen to you.

One of Tracy's key messages is that before anything else each day, we should do the thing that we dislike the most, as it could be one of the most important to accomplish. As a result, you will be more efficient with everything else.

If instead you are thinking all day about the frog that you still must eat, nothing tastes quite right. That's because you are anticipating the terror on your tongue. Everything seems sweeter, more delicious, once you know you won't have to endure that frog.

For example, you may enjoy exercise once you get started, but you may not want to crawl out of your warm bed and get dressed for the gym. So you start procrastinating. You lie there, fiddle with your smartphone, check out your social networks—anything to put off getting up. But if you just throw off those covers and eat that frog, you'll get to the gym, and you'll actually enjoy the treadmill as you exercise and listen to music.

That happens at work, too. It happens in everything in life. I believe that procrastination leads to negative thinking and even depression—and I know that from personal experience. Worrying about the frog, you fill your days with the daily minutiae that prevent you from seeing and pursuing your true passions. As you think, "Oh, no, I still have to eat that frog," you begin telling yourself bad stories. It taints your thinking all day.

I confess that I don't eat my frog every day—nobody does—but when I do and finally tackle the most difficult matters, I have a sense of fulfillment and clarity that liberates me to work on the other things. The day seems lighter now that I have done the tough stuff.

LESSON 7

ASKING IS POWERFUL

I have a big admiration for Jack Canfield, coauthor of the best-selling *Chicken Soup* book series. He basically invites people to open up and share their stories, and the books speak to people from many walks of life. When you read other people's stories, you see hope and help for yourself.

In his book *The Success Principles*, Canfield discusses the 64 best practices for success. They are about how you can find your life purpose, follow your passion, and be bold. And one that resonated particularly with me was the principle of "*Ask, ask, ask.*" Rather than presume the answer is no, simply ask. Things can get better. You might ask for simple things such as an upgrade on your flight, or you might ask for a discount at the store.

We tend to be afraid of asking. Asking may be uncomfortable. Asking a question may make you look bad, or seeking a favor may feel uncomfortable, but I have discovered that once you rise above that feeling, the worst that happens is that you hear no. Often, you are better off than you were. It's not only about big things; it's also about little things. If you become proficient with little things, you will be able to apply it to larger things that can bring big returns.

You may feel weak asking someone for a favor, but just do it. If you ask for a discount, you frequently will get one. But if you don't bother to ask, certainly you are not going to get one. If you ask for a favor, you very well may get that favor. If you don't ask, of course you are not going to get it.

Jack Canfield spoke at an entrepreneur event in Monterrey, Mexico, that I attended. I brought along my *Success Principles* book, which is tattered and underlined. I had another meeting, and I was not going to be able to make it for the book signature time. I found Jack before his workshop and I said, "Jack, I've been wanting to meet you for so many years. I've read this book, and it really had a big impact on my life. You have great principles there, but the principle '*ask, ask, ask*' has really paid for the book many times. So I am applying this principle right now: Will you please sign my book now, even if it is not the signature time?" And of course he did.

You must put that principle into practice. I recently negotiated better payment terms with one of my strategic partners. I said, "Okay, we're taking this inventory, but I need you to give me good payment terms to show my own shareholders. Can you help me on that?" The answer: "Yes, of course, let's go ahead."

It's a discipline. Not only can you ask for things, but you also should ask questions in order to keep on learning. You need to do it, even though for many people asking doesn't come easily. In that way, it's like the principle of "eat that frog." If you ask a question in front of a group, you may feel ignorant, but many times you may find out that others had that same question too, and you end up triggering a higher level of trust among everyone.

LESSON 8

IF YOU WANT TO HAVE FRIENDS, START BY BEING ONE

I finished my sushi and opened the fortune cookie, and this was the message: "The only way to have a friend is to be one." I have since kept that slip of paper as a reminder of this important principle.

"How can you be a good friend?" I asked myself. And what I have learned through the years is this: To be a good friend, one must be willing to open up. Be vulnerable. Make yourself look vulnerable. Don't pretend; be authentic.

Everybody has problems. Many people pretend to have a great life, but there's a saying: "We see the houses, but we're not aware of the mortgages behind them." Be willing to talk about your "mortgage" as well as your house. That way, you will get other people to also talk about their "mortgage," and maybe you can get ideas from each other.

I have always received much in return when I open up with other people to talk about my challenges.

True friends share themselves thoroughly. They share their victories, but they also share their fears and their worries. That's what binds them together more deeply. If you are only sharing a piece of yourself, your victories, no one really knows what you are going through, and therefore they cannot help you with it.

At the beginning of the EO forum in 2009, we were six strangers. We were not yet friends, but the methodology of the EO forum and the protocol helped us to open up. It is all about sharing experiences, not about giving recommendations.

Peer groups help you open up. There should be a code of honor that holds everyone to the rule of whatever is said there, stays there—this will encourage you to open up. The more you do so, the more others follow suit. I have seen that process of maturing in my EO forum. At first in the EO forum, we would talk about rather superficial stuff. Then somebody would open up and tell something deeper, and that would set the pace for the others. After five years, we have gotten to the point where we can open up about very deep things.

You have to share; you have to take the step of letting others understand what's really going on with you. That way they can help you, and then they will open up themselves.

Many people come from a culture or a generation in which it is not typical to open up. Most of us were taught from childhood to keep our feelings and opinions to ourselves, but you pay the penalty after a while for that. Your world starts to close in. When you open up and when you actually become a friend—then the world inside you becomes much bigger.

In the EO forum, we are trained to listen. We give one another updates on the best and the worst things that have happened to us in business, in personal life, and in family life. Everybody must listen. It's prohibited to look at your smartphone or computer. It's prohibited to do side talking. When you listen to others, they listen to you. They return the favor.

In business, if you are able to listen to the prospective customer and understand his problem and reflect it to him, this brings you closer to closing the sale. If you don't listen and the prospect does not feel understood, your greatest proposal will go nowhere.

Everyone should learn at an early age that if you want to be good friends with someone, you must share yourself. You make yourself vulnerable, in other words. You hear others out. That's where friendships begin, and that's where personal growth begins. As we say in EO: "The more you give, the more you get."

LESSON 9

MAKE NETWORKING A HABIT

Shortly after I founded my business in 1996, I went with my family on a vacation to Philadelphia. At the time, I was selling a software package called Solomon. I looked up who was in the business of selling Solomon and noticed somebody in Delaware, south of Philadelphia. I sent an email to that person, saying, "I'm from Mexico. I just got into the Solomon business. I understand that you are very successful with Solomon. Can we have lunch together?" He responded, "Yes, by all means."

While we were in Philadelphia, I drove down to meet him for lunch. I told him about how Solomon was doing in Mexico. Solomon was very new in Mexico. We talked about joint opportunities—and he invited me to the annual kickoff meeting of his company two weeks later at his Dallas office.

"I would like to invite you to fly up to Dallas and to get acquainted," he said. "My brother's running the Dallas office with another partner. Just get acquainted with each other, because you are close by, and you could do projects together." So I made arrangements to fly to Dallas.

We started doing some small projects for Mexican customers together, and a year later, one of the partners from the Dallas office, who is now a good friend of mine, sent me an email: "Hey, can you help me a little bit with the Spanish version of Solomon? Can you send me the Spanish overlay for that?" I emailed it to him. A week later, he called me: "Nicolas, do you have a consultant that you could send to Caracas, Venezuela, to do a project?" I agreed and went with another consultant for a week to do some work there.

The company we were working with had locations all over Latin America and became one of our largest customers ever over a period of at least five years. But that did not all happen immediately. The dividends came over the ensuing several years. That's the nature and the power of networking. I didn't start out expecting anything, but it came.

I plant seeds. I love networking. In 2010, after the new CEO joined the company, most of my time was devoted to networking. One-third of the new projects that we signed in 2010 came from my networking. But they didn't come from the mixers I went to that year. They came from the relationships that I had developed in previous years.

Some people attend networking events and mixers and expect to get business deals there. But that's not the point. You might get a deal, if you are lucky. But, in my experience, expecting to go to one networking event and get immediate business is like expecting to go to the gym one morning and be in good shape that very same day. Or expecting to read one book and know it all.

When you network, you are building relationships. Things will develop from there. You need to give everything and expect nothing, and the magic will happen over time. You can't force it. The goal of networking isn't to immediately consummate the deal. The idea is to build relationships.

Whenever I visit somewhere new, I see if I can contact somebody. When I travel, I try to visit the local EO chapter or the local representative of one of the brands that I work with. It's my nature. I'm relationship-oriented. I send birthday wishes and share articles on my social networks that others might find useful.

However, when it comes to running a business, I surround myself with task-oriented people. They will handle the operational details, and I will handle the relationships. We need one another. That's why networking is so important. We bring our skills together.

There is a principle I read in a book called *The World's Worst Networker* that says "Nobody is a nobody." That means you can get a good referral from anybody.

I like the concept offered by *BNI*, a major worldwide networking organization that recommends people to each other. It doesn't matter if you are a high-powered businessman, a gardener, or a barber. Everybody has the potential of providing good referrals.

I experience the benefits of my networking efforts over and over again.

LESSON 10

DON'T FALL IN LOVE WITH YOUR FIRST IDEAS

In late 2013, I went to a workshop with Alex Osterwalder, creator of the Business Model Canvas, who coauthored the famous book, *Business Model Generation*, which I will include in the next section among the tools for business. I am passionate about that concept, and it always helps me get clarity about the operation of my own business ventures.

We were taught about "*design thinking*," where the idea is to start thinking more like a designer, even if you are a businessman, and test things out first at a prototype level. At the workshop, Osterwalder asked us to design a business model for a fictitious company. Once we had designed it, he told us to crumple up the business model and throw it to the center of the room. Why would we do that? He told us that the first principle of design thinking is this: don't you ever fall in love with your first idea. Challenge your ideas.

You need to get feedback from other people. Don't just remain with the first idea. The name of my IT company is Fillgap. We have been in the market for almost 18 years, and our business model has evolved from being a software reseller for a single company to developing a portfolio of product and service solutions that add value to other resellers and end-users. At first, I was going to call it Gapfill, because we were going to fill the gaps that customers have in enterprise software packages. My brother advised me, however, that Gapfill would be hard to pronounce and suggested that Fillgap would sound better. Today it is a registered mark, and it is not about developing the gaps for software anymore. We have redefined the purpose of our company to fill the gaps that keep businesses from growing, and that entails a much bigger vision.

LESSON 11

KNOW WHEN TO QUIT

Quitting something can be hard, like "eating a very big frog." But it can be worthwhile. Knowing when to quit is an art rather than a science. There are many examples throughout history where people let go of something and kept their minds open—which made room for better things to come along. Paradoxically, history is also full of examples where people stuck to their ideas and finally succeeded.

Mike Michalowicz is the best-selling author of *The Pumpkin Plan* and *Profit First,* among other books. He has developed coaching and training programs for entrepreneurs, and we do business with him and his organizations as part of our coaching portfolio. He is also a mentor to us. At a critical moment in our coaching business, he recommended that we read a book by Seth Godin called *The Dip: A Little Book That Teaches You When to Quit (and When to Stick).*

We read the book, and it motivated us to keep on going with our coaching business. In other words, we decided to stick. However, that very same book made me decide the opposite with my IT company.

We had a business unit that was constantly losing money and causing us headaches. After investing heavily, we managed to produce important revenues but without making any profits—and worse, without being able to make our customers happy.

I said to my partner, "This is keeping us from concentrating on things that are more productive or better. Why don't we negotiate an exit strategy with all the stakeholders and hand over the business unit to somebody else?"

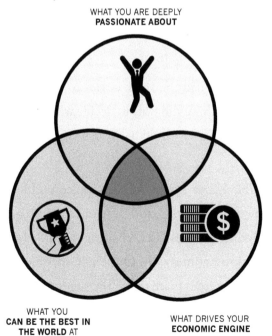

WHAT YOU ARE DEEPLY
PASSIONATE ABOUT

WHAT YOU
**CAN BE THE BEST IN
THE WORLD** AT

WHAT DRIVES YOUR
ECONOMIC ENGINE

To make the final decision, I used the three circles that Jim Collins uses in the book *Good to Great*. These three circles are: (1) Can you be the best at what you are doing? (2) Are you passionate about it? (3) Are you making money?

We evaluated that business unit, and we confirmed that we were not being profitable there. Nor were we passionate about that unit anymore. And we could not be the best at that business either. It was just consuming a lot of resources and time. So, making sure our customers were safe, we took a financial hit and handed the unit over to somebody else. It was painful, but it freed up resources, time, and energy, allowing us to focus on more productive initiatives for our business long term.

Had we applied the three circles to our coaching business (which we did not) to decide weather to quit or stick, the answer would have been yes for the three of them.

In *Think and Grow Rich*, Napoleon Hill says, "A quitter never wins and a winner never quits." Seth Godin, decades later, challenges that. He says, "Winners sometimes quit. Quitters sometimes win." And both statements are right! The slight difference is that according to Godin, "Winners just quit the right stuff at the right time."

The message here is to be open to the possibility of quitting when things are not going as expected. Even if you decide to continue, the thinking process of whether to quit or to stick is invaluable, and you will resume your endeavor with renewed energy.

LESSON 12

USE SMART GOALS
AND RHYTHM

It is said that a goal is a dream with a deadline, and it was my brother Tomas who first made me aware of the term "SMART goals" at a moment when I was struggling to set and follow up on some personal priorities. Since then, I have noticed that numerous experts and coaches use this term as a standard to help set a goal, validate it, and follow up on it.

SMART is an acronym that guides the setting of goals in fields such as business management, project management, employee performance management, and personal development. There are different versions for what it stands for. My preferred one is the following:

S = Specific (concrete, tangible)

M = Measurable (how you'll know you reached the goal, a tangible result)

A = Achievable (something you are capable of doing)

R = Relevant (something that matters to you)

T = Time-limited (something to be reached by a specific date)

These are examples of SMART goals:

1. I will lose 20 pounds by the end of this year.

2. I will have a minimum of five new paying clients by *<a specific month>*.

3. I will create a first draft of my business card and brochure by *<a specific date>*.

These are not SMART goals:

1. I am going to be healthier.

2. I am going to be rich.

3. I will work on marketing.

I believe in using the SMART criteria as a guideline rather than as a nonnegotiable standard. The SMARTer the goal, the easier it will be to follow up on it. The less SMART a goal is, the more it becomes an aspirational goal. Not all goals can be set to be 100 percent SMART, especially long-term goals where you don't have all the information.

Long-term aspirational goals are, however, still necessary and extremely important to set the direction for our growth and fulfillment of our potential. John Maxwell, internationally renowned leadership expert, suggests that when you focus on growth rather than only on goals, you will most likely hit and exceed your goals anyway.

Once a goal is defined, you need to break it down into the required milestones or activities to achieve it. The level of detail depends on each person and on each goal, but it must be detailed enough to follow through and not so detailed as to be overwhelming.

From my Gazelles International certification, I have learned how to use the concept of *rhythm* to create a habit of following up on your goals: applying yearly, quarterly, monthly, weekly, and even daily checkpoints. Each checkpoint has its specific purpose and items to watch for, and being consistent with the follow up is a critical component for successfully reaching a goal.

In the next section, we will have the opportunity to go into further detail on how to make use of goals and rhythm in your personal life and in your business.

SECTION THREE

THE THREE CHALLENGES

" Entrepreneurs see opportunities where others see hurdles, taking risks where others seek shelter," says Michael Bloomberg, business magnate and former New York City mayor.

A true entrepreneur brings ideas to life, aligning the right people and resources, and also makes sure the idea stays alive. Entrepreneurs need to be humble enough to either step aside when the business has outgrown their skills or proactively invest in their professional and personal growth, hence staying current with the growing demands of their company. They may also need to bring in people with different skill sets. It's all quite challenging.

We normally think of an entrepreneur as a person who launches a company, but an entrepreneur can also be an "intrapreneur." An intrapreneur is an employee of a corporation, a nonprofit, an educational institution, or even a government agency. According to Alex Osterwalder, a component of entrepreneurship has become a necessity for large companies to reinvent themselves for the future.

"All human beings are entrepreneurs," according to Muhammad Yunus, the Bangladeshi economist who won the Nobel Peace Prize for pioneering the concept of microfinance. "When we used to live in the caves, we were all self-employed, looking for our own food, and this is how the history of humanity started. Later on, when civilization arrived, we were all labeled as employees, and we forgot that we are entrepreneurs."

In his book *Job Shift: How to Prosper in a Workplace without Jobs,* William Bridges wrote, back in the early

1990s, that employees should see themselves as a company. You should assess your strengths and assets to see how you could become a "company" offering services to your current employer. If you lose that job, you have a specialty you can offer to others.

"Entrepreneurs are inventors who are constantly asking themselves: 'What is missing here?'" says Michael Gerber, author of *The E-Myth*.

Being a great entrepreneur also requires being a great leader. In his book *The 5 Levels of Leadership*, John Maxwell explains that true leadership isn't about having a certain job or title. In fact, being chosen for a position is only the first of the five levels he describes of becoming an effective leader. In essence, to create true following, we must not only achieve results for our organization, but we must also build a team that produces results and in which new leaders emerge.

On my journey, I have encountered many other entrepreneurs who are going through the same challenges as I have faced. They are striving to learn their strengths and weaknesses, develop and share a vision, and put it into action.

"So What Will Your Book Be About?"

As I began to conceive the idea for this book, colleagues, family, and friends would ask me the obvious question: "So what will your book be about?" I responded, "Well, because of my own experiences, I am very passionate about the impact your personal life has in business and vice versa."

In prior years I had contributed a variety of articles to different publications on this topic, and I had thoroughly covered it during my keynotes. The question, however, led me to dig in deeper into what I had experienced and what I had learned.

Through the years, I have tried to identify the greatest challenges that an entrepreneur faces. In doing so, I have found three challenges that are at the heart of what this book is about. I have distilled them from my readings, the workshops I have taken, the conferences I have been in, personal life and business challenges, and from the experiences I have exchanged with my entrepreneur peers and my coaching peers. And these challenges are:

1. The challenge of mastering yourself first

2. The challenge of mastering your company's direction

3. The challenge of mastering consistent performance for your company

In this section, we will take a closer look at each of these challenges, and I will introduce you to a set of the most important tools to help you overcome them. My goal here is to make you aware of these tools and of additional sources for further detail. I have put together diverse ideas into a system that I am confident will work for you as you strive to improve your life in business.

CHALLENGE 1: MASTERING YOURSELF FIRST

We have 60,000 thoughts a day, and it can be difficult to control them—but you can control how you feel about them. You can emphasize the positive thoughts, and in doing so you will attract positive things into your life.

I first learned about the "Law of Attraction" from the movie *The Secret*. It made me think of Henry Ford's assertion that if he somehow lost his fortune, he was confident that he could regain it soon. He had a sense of awareness of himself and the sources of his success. I knew that I needed such self-awareness in my own life.

How had I made the law of attraction work for me in the past, without even being aware of it? How would I make it work for me now? How would I use it to build toward better things? How could I find a repeatable pattern? I realized that the first things I needed to have were peace of mind and clarity about what I wanted to do and what and whom I wanted to attract.

Once you have peace of mind and you have clarity about what you want, you need a plan to know where you are going. Then you need to have faith, and you need to take action. You can have the nicest plan, but if you don't start working, it will all remain as just a plan. That is how the law of attraction had worked for me in the past, and it had led me to success.

John Assaraf, one of the people featured in *The Secret*, is the author of *Having It All: Achieving Your Life's Goals and Dreams*. In one chapter, he takes a look at the brain's reticular activation system, which processes all the sensory information it receives. He writes, "The RAS asks itself one simple question: Is this something that's important to my owner?" If it's unessential or irrelevant information, the RAS won't make you aware of it.

"That's the secret of *The Secret*," I thought as I took in his words. There are many aspects to the law of attraction, but for me, the reticular activation system is the key issue. Assaraf gives this example: Let's say you are thinking about buying a certain kind of car. Have you ever noticed how you suddenly start seeing that make and model everywhere?

We need to set our reticular activation system to start seeing opportunities coming toward us. As people and organizations become aware of their vision, and as they gain peace of mind and clarity, those opportunities will seem to be everywhere.

We focus on what we need. Something can be there for us all along, but we notice it only when it becomes important to us. In business and in life, things begin to reveal themselves once we attain that clarity on what we want and where we want to go.

"You must know yourself to grow yourself," says John Maxwell in his book *The 15 Invaluable Laws of Growth*. In learning to master myself, I have consolidated a set of considerations into a process and have listed other recommendations that I believe you will find helpful. They include:

1. Your lifeline chart

2. An attitude of gratitude

3. Your "bucket list"

4. Your personal values

5. Your life purpose and mission

6. Your life wheel: slicing your life for better understanding

7. Your life assessment

8. Re-imagining your life

9. Taking responsibility for your life

1. YOUR LIFELINE CHART

Becoming self-aware doesn't happen all at once. It's not as if you wake up and say, "Okay, today I'm going to become aware of my personal values and my life purpose." You first need to warm up.

Think of your life as like a movie. Perhaps consider it in five-year stretches: What were the ups and downs during those five years? You can view your life as a whole, and you can make a graphic.

On your lifeline chart, list the years of your life on one axis, on the X. The Y axis will be a scale of one to ten; for each year of your life, give yourself a grade by marking a point on that scale. The grade reflects the degree to which you feel that was a good or a bad year for you. Then draw a line connecting the points. You can either draw one line to view your life as a whole, or you might draw three lines for personal, family, and professional.

Personal

Family

Professional

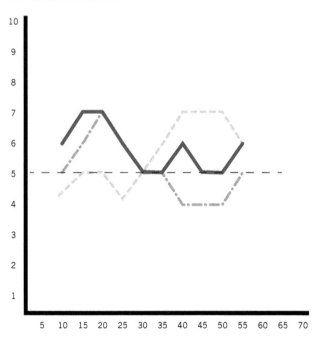

Personal Satisfaction Level

Age

The beauty of this exercise is that it stirs your memories. You will find yourself remembering the good and the bad. Write them down. That will help you to get a perspective on what went well and not so well. The graph helps you to see your peaks and the valleys. We all have them. It gives you a visual, and when you write down the specifics, it seems as if you are scripting the movie of your life story.

This exercise helps you to think about what you have accomplished, where you may have gone wrong, and where you may have made missteps. You will have time to make corrections. You will have time to do more of what you do well while doing less of the rest. And most importantly, you will feel inspired.

2. AN ATTITUDE OF GRATITUDE

To be grateful, it is said, is good for your health, which in itself is a good reason to become aware of the positive things that have come your way.

I pray almost every night with my daughter, who now is ten years old. When she was a little girl, we used to say a prayer and ask God to take care of us in whatever situation we were living through.

But one night, out of the blue, she began a prayer of gratitude. She was thankful for what she already had. With her prayer, my little daughter opened my eyes: we need to say thank you first.

Once you start recognizing what's been given to you, then you feel very grateful. You stop dwelling on the downs, and you start thinking about the ups. To emphasize the positive first is a good practice in prayer—and it's a good practice as you plan the steps you will take in life. Don't begin by emphasizing the things you don't have, but instead, count your blessings first.

3. YOUR BUCKET LIST

Once you are done counting your blessings, start working on your "bucket list." Think about the things you want to do—whether personal, professional, or whatever—and just write them down. You may recall *The Bucket List* movie with Jack Nicholson and Morgan Freeman, who play two men facing death who go on a quest to do the things they always wanted to experience before they "kick the bucket."

Your own bucket list will consist of the essentials that you want to accomplish. You can chart those on your lifeline graph. It's as if you are projecting your life into the future. The years ahead hold great promise as you pursue your bucket list. As we move forward, you are going to see some tools that help you build on that bucket list.

4. YOUR PERSONAL VALUES

Your personal values are the ideals and the views that determine what really matters to you and how you live your life. They represent the filter through which you make your decisions. Values are personal guidelines for your life and go beyond moral principles, which may also be part of your set of values.

Being aware of your personal values and living according to them will provide you with piece of mind, direction, and fulfillment. We should also take our personal values into consideration when we choose whom we associate with, both in our personal and business lives.

For example, some people place a high value on the pursuit of excellence. Others uphold such values as commitment, respect, generosity, or acceptance. Further examples of generally accepted personal values are available from different sources including life coaching professionals, specialized publications, and a variety of personal development and management books.

The first time that I became conscious of the application of personal values was when I read the book *Life Manual* by Peter H. Thomas who suggests considering your set of values as one of your "personal navigational dashboard." That is when I began writing the first draft of my personal values and to understand how they influence my decisions and the course in the different areas my life.

A few years later, at an EO retreat, one of our peers facilitated a values discovery exercise based on a chapter of the book *Bury My Heart at Conference Room B* by management consultant Stan Slap. I found it to be a great resource for anyone who wants to identify his or her values.

I also remember reading an article by Darren Hardy, publisher of *Success Magazine*, explaining that your personal values are reflected in your calendar and your account statement. How are you spending your time; how are you spending your money? If you see that you spend a lot on books, you probably value learning. If you see that you spend a lot of time being with friends, you value relationships. Take a look at your own calendar and spending records, and you well might see patterns that you hadn't recognized.

If you like social networks and are active on a regular basis, go back and review your posts, your "likes" and your "shares" (from other people's posts), and see if you can find one or more patterns. We tend to post, like, and share the things that we care about and value.

You may also use your life wheel, as explained in the next exercise, to reflect on how you spend time, energy, and money. That will also give you a hint on what is important for you and help you identify your values.

I found a very good explanation on the extreme importance of becoming aware and living by your values in the German personal health book called *Lebe Balance* (Life Balance). This book was coauthored, based on a strong scientific foundation, by four mental health professionals who specialize on topics such as self-management, stress management, burnout prevention, depression, and sleep disorders. They explain that modern psychology is giving more and more importance to the topic of personal values, because of the impact it has on living a meaningful, fulfilling, and emotionally healthy life.

They also explain that, in these modern times, we are being exposed to an overwhelmingly large array of options to decide on and that it is our nature as human beings to be seduced by our emotions when we have to make a decision. Therefore, not being aware of your personal values to base your decisions on poses the risk of deciding for things that may satisfy your short term but may not be your best option for the long term.

Finally, in order to build a deeper awareness of your personal values and to implement them in your life, they suggest to not only identify what values are important to you but to also write up your own slogans (value by value) with personal examples of why they are important for you. You can also do it the other way around by starting to write slogans of what is important to you and, later on, relate them to generally accepted values.

An indicator that you are living according to your values is when you experience peace of mind. If you constantly lack such peace, it's a good idea to revisit your values and actions.

5. YOUR LIFE PURPOSE AND MISSION

As I have emphasized, everything and everybody has a purpose for being here. We come with a purpose, and our first mission is to discover it. After discovering your purpose, you assign yourself one or more missions during life to fulfill that purpose. It took me way too long to become aware that we all have a purpose and then to discover it. I was 44 when I discovered my purpose. If you are younger than I was, don't wait as long as I did. If you are as old or older than I was, it is better late than never.

A friend who is cofounder of an asset management firm in Mexico recently told me: "My purpose is to have a positive impact on others. When I discovered that, I chose a mission and drew an action plan to have that impact."

How do you connect with your purpose? A lot of help is available, and much has been written on the topic, but I would narrow it down to three steps, based on my experiences and studies.

The first step is to become aware of your natural gifts and talents. To approach this, I suggest that you reflect on situations during your life where you have experienced personal success and fulfillment.

The second step is to live out of love. I have learned that all emotions can be reduced to two basic ones: love and fear. Everything we think and do is out of love or out of fear. We can come closer to understanding our life purpose by becoming aware of the things that we do out of love and the things that we do out of fear. When we do things out of love, we experience fulfillment and the "flow" that I discussed in section 2 on lessons learned.

The third step in connecting with your purpose is to think of ways to make these gifts and talents available to others. In his book, *The Purpose Driven Life*, Rick Warren explains that when you use your gifts to serve others, the generosity of God flows through you. Thinking about ways to serve others based on your gifts will also set the groundwork to define your life mission (or missions) as I explained before.

6. YOUR LIFE WHEEL: SLICING YOUR LIFE FOR BETTER UNDERSTANDING

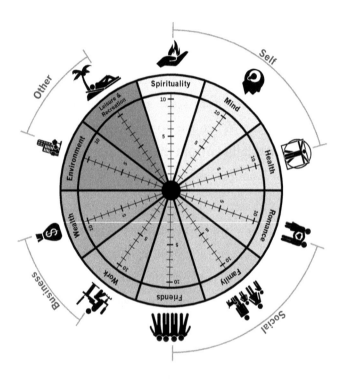

The life wheel is a valuable tool for assessing your life, and one that coaches often use to help their clients become clear about where they are standing in their life. As opposed to the lifeline chart, in which you can see the "movie" of your life over the years, the life wheel provides a snapshot of any given moment.

I divided my wheel into ten slices to indicate various areas of my life, and I believe that this is the standard that every entrepreneur should use: (1) spirituality, (2) mind, (3) body, (4) romance, (5) family, (6) friends, (7) work, (8) wealth, (9) environment, and (10) leisure and recreation.

The first three slices are related to a sense of self, such as spirituality, character, personal and intellectual growth, and health. Slices four to six are the social ones, and they are obvious. Seven is work. Eight is wealth and personal finances. Nine is one's environment and community. And ten refers to things one enjoys doing to recharge, either alone or with others, such as hobbies and travel.

After constructing my wheel, I asked myself: "So where is my business on this wheel?" Well, my business resides in two of the slices: "work" and "wealth."

What I wish to emphasize here is you are not your business, and the business is not you. Many people fail to understand that. If, from the "work" point of view, you are not the right person or don't possess the appropriate skills to lead or run it, or you simply have lost interest in what you are doing, you could make poor decisions that put your "wealth" at risk. You will need to have the maturity and the courage to say, "I'm not the person to run this business anymore. I need to find somebody to help me run this business. Or I need to learn, acquire new skills, and grow according to the circumstances."

You need to view yourself as a shareholder of your business, not as the business itself. You must do what is best for it, which means that if you don't grow and adjust personally and professionally to the demanding circumstances of a business, you might have to open yourself to the possibility of "firing" yourself. You'll be out of a job and you will have to find something else to do inside or outside your company, but you will be protecting your business and, hence, your wealth.

Another critical consideration here is the way you compensate yourself and other co-owners in your company. The golden rule to follow is that you get salary, bonuses, and other awards for what you do as an employee (the "work" slice of your life wheel), and you get dividends for the amount of equity you have as a shareholder (the "wealth" slice of your life wheel).

When it comes to your business, always make sure that you draw a line between your work and your personal wealth. This line is, for me, the principle of corporate governance. You must make sure that your business is protected, even from yourself. Good corporate governance begins with understanding the principle of watching out for the interest of the shareholders. You may be the owner, but the business must be well-run. Your personal wealth depends on it. If you do not respect that principle, you could drive your business into bankruptcy. This is why companies, no matter how small they are, should have a board of advisors or at least one external advisor to help them remain objective and accountable.

7. YOUR LIFE ASSESSMENT

At the end of every year, I sit down by myself in a quiet and inspiring place, and I look at my life. I go slice by slice and ask myself the following questions: What does success look like? What were my achievements, and what were my setbacks? Then I consider the good happenings and the bad happenings, which are external factors. These are things I was not responsible for causing, but I ask myself: Was I prepared for that? How did I react to it?

Then for each slice, I consider the things I need to do more of, the things I need to do less of, and the things I must start and stop doing. I also ask myself what am I doing on a day-to-day basis out of love, and what am I doing out of fear? Am I staying in a relationship, or in a business, or in a friendship out of fear or out of love?

Another important question: What do I take for granted that is important? A Jewish rabbi once visited our EO forum and gave us the definition of happiness: "Happiness is being aware of all those things that you have that are important for you but you normally take for granted." For example, he said, if you lost an eye, how much would you be willing to pay to recover your eye? Whatever it takes. But how many times are you aware that you have eyes? Or that you can walk? Or that you have a house? Or that you have your kids?

It's a bit different than the gratitude list, where you brainstorm about everything for which you are grateful. These are the things we often don't think about. And yet we really must be grateful that we have eyes, and can see, and can walk, and have a house, and our kids, and a job, and good friends. Many times we take those things for granted and don't think about them as we should.

Then, slice by slice, I also put in some lessons learned and whether I need to attend to any outstanding matters.

Lastly, I give a grade to each slice, on a scale from zero to ten, based on how satisfied I am with each area of my life.

The grading scale begins at the center of the wheel and goes out to the rim. For each segment, you put a dot where your grade falls, and then you connect those dots. The resulting shape is a picture of how satisfied and fulfilled you feel in your life.

You may also want to repeat the grading exercise using additional criteria, such as how much attention you devoted to each slice. Hence, the life wheel can also give you a snapshot of where you are placing your attention, and it can also help you to see what you really value.

2.- Connect the dots

3.- Fill the shape

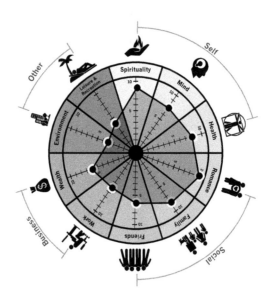

8. RE-IMAGINING YOUR LIFE

Consider each of those slices, and think about what you aspire being, doing, and having in your life. These are your long-term wishes and dreams, also known as aspirations.

Think of it this way: If you were writing a letter to Santa Claus, what would you ask him to give you? Most people in Mexico celebrate Christmas, so that resonates with my audiences when I speak to groups. Just let your imagination and your dreams flow. Slice by slice, think of your ideal world and what you would desire from it. These are your aspirations, and they are normally long-term—somewhere from 5 to 25 years.

9. TAKING RESPONSIBILITY FOR YOUR LIFE

After I encourage my audience either at keynotes or workshops to write their "Letter to Santa Claus," I tell them: "Now it is time to become Santa Clauses ourselves and take responsibility."

First, I suggest they ask themselves this: "What kind of person do I need to become to attract the things I aspire?" Think about your ideal traits, skills, character, and physical condition. "Success is what you attract by the person you become," according to Jim Rohn, who was a rags-to-riches entrepreneur and motivational speaker. We tend to forget the importance of working on our own character and traits. But this is something we cannot risk forgetting.

You can do that by focusing on each of the slices of your life wheel and asking that key question: What do I need to become? If I want to become a gold medal bicyclist, then I need to practice so many hours a day. If I want to become an author, I need to write one hour a day.

After you have identified your aspirations and become aware of the person you need to become, you need to set priorities. Of all the ten slices, where do you need to focus first?

A way of becoming clear about your priorities is to think about two things:

1)   Which slice could you work on, even if it takes a big effort and a considerable amount of time and resources, so that by improving it, it would have the biggest impact on the rest of the wheel?

2) On which slice could you apply some easy-to-implement activities that could have a big short-term benefit that would motivate you and give you energy to work toward your aspirations?

After you set priorities, you set the goals. Your goals are milestones toward fulfilling who you need to become and your aspirations. Remember to make your goals SMART and to break them down into activities as discussed in section 2.

OTHER CONSIDERATIONS

- Think on paper: Write down your thoughts during this process. Writing it all down will better stimulate your reticular activation system (RAS) to set your mind to things that are important. This is mandatory. And write it on paper, not on the computer—you can use the computer later. Go to the park. Go to the beach. Go to wherever you feel inspired, and pull out your pen and paper. You can't remember everything that you need to do. You have

to put it down so that you have a checklist
to work with.

- Get an accountability partner: Your
  partner could be a coach or a counselor.
  Or you might be part of an accountability
  or peer group. There must be no conflict
  of interest, so this should not be your
  business partner. Nor should your partner
  be a close friend or a relative or your
  older brother or your spouse (unless you
  are working on family planning). Your
  accountability partner will help you think
  through the process and give you feedback
  and also can help you follow up on things.
  For example, I found an accountability
  partnership through my EO forum, our
  group of seven who get together monthly
  to talk about our businesses and personal
  lives. You can have a partner for your life
  as a whole or more than one partner for
  particular slices of your life. John Maxwell
  suggests getting an accountability partner
  for the areas of your life where you are not
  disciplined enough.

- Follow through with rhythm: Your self-assessment and planning exercise should be continuous, not once and done. I suggest doing the complete exercise annually before the year ends and review it quarterly. Depending on the priority you give to each area of your life, you can monitor your goals quarterly or monthly and follow up on your activities weekly or daily.

CHALLENGE 2: MASTERING YOUR COMPANY'S DIRECTION

Mike Wazowski and Sully were the best in Monstropolis at getting kids to scream—but those screams were getting ever harder to produce. The monsters needed to bottle those screams to generate electricity for the city. What to do?

In the Disney film *Monsters Inc.*, times were changing—kids didn't scare easily anymore. Some of the monsters resorted to nasty experiments to get them to scream louder. But others stumbled upon a solution: They could get more energy by making kids laugh—and so they redesigned their business model around laughter.

The monsters lacked a common sense of purpose and perspective. Some held fast to the ways of the past. They were determined to squeeze out whatever screams they could. Meanwhile, other monsters moved forward to a solution.

Whether or not the producers intended it that way, I see the movie as an allegory for business innovation. It has some fundamental lessons for entrepreneurs. The monsters needed alignment to get them all on the same page so that their enterprise could do best in changing times. They needed a shared vision.

GROUND RULES FOR BUILDING A SHARED VISION

The need for a shared vision is central to business success. To master that vision, you need to follow some rules for working effectively with stakeholders toward a common interest:

- Create a safe environment for everybody. In his book *The Five Dysfunctions of a Team,* Patrick Lencioni discusses that the first requirement to have a functional team is trust. And by trust he means that team members need to trust one another enough to be vulnerable. This way they know they can admit weakness, take risks, ask "stupid" questions, or even fail, without being punished.

- Think like an investor. An investor's major concern is whether the company will do well. All other considerations are secondary to that. If you and your leadership team think like employees, your personal interests get in the way— matters of salary or power. They present a conflict of interest. When all participants think like investors, however, they share the same interest—and that is the company's profitability and sustainability.

- Understand that the "we" is more important than the "me." My father taught me that. His consulting company consisted primarily of just himself, a secretary, and some temps. But whenever he would present a proposal to a client, he would say, "we" and "us," as in: "We are pleased to submit this proposal to you."

- You should take a "win-win" approach with your stakeholders. That is one of my core values that I have emphasized within my company.

- A company needs to agree on a common language and terminology. For example, the company Target has adopted a word in all its stores in the United States to refer to their customers as "guests."

- Be hard on the problems, but be soft on the people. Disagreements are inevitable. Be tough about tackling the issues that you are trying to solve, but be soft on your other stakeholders sitting around the table.

In addition to that general advice, you will need to address several fundamental considerations as you work to set the direction of your company. I present them here in a logical order, although you can focus first on whichever seems of priority to you:

1. Your company's core values

2. The core purpose of your business

3. Purpose, vision, and mission statements

4. The stage your business is in

5. Understanding and building alignment with your stakeholders

6. Your business model

7. Your target customer

8. Your company's story

Let's examine each of those considerations.

1. YOUR COMPANY'S CORE VALUES

In the last chapter, "Mastering Yourself First," we discussed personal values and the importance of being aware of them. The same happens in business. Like people, many businesses are not aware of how important it is to operate according to core values.

Core values are the foundation of your company's culture. This is why they are first in this section, even before the core purpose of your business. Core values are the rules and boundaries under which your company will operate and make decisions. You also want to make sure that you associate with others who share your core values.

In their Harvard Business Review article "Building Your Company's Vision," Jim Collins and Jerry Porras define core values as "the handful of guiding principles by which a company navigates."

Verne Harnish, founder of Gazelles, compares the core values of a company with the principles you would use to raise your children: you need a handful of rules, you need to repeat them often, and you need to live by them yourself. Verne is the author of the best-selling book *Mastering the Rockefeller Habits* and the major revision that came out recently, *Scaling Up*, in which he gives examples of how companies have discerned and effectively developed their core values.

The general rule is that companies should not have more than five to seven core values and that those values should be communicated often, through posters and stories that illustrate how the company is living by them. These are timeless guiding principles. To stay true to its values, your company should be willing to sacrifice, such as taking a financial hit, firing an employee, dropping a product line, or even going out of a market.

In February of 2014, for example, CVS Pharmacy announced its decision to stop selling tobacco products. The company estimated that it would lose approximately $2 billion in revenues on an annual basis from this decision. But when you read the company's core purpose, which is "helping people on their path to better health," and its core values, "innovation, collaboration, caring, integrity, and accountability," the decision makes perfect sense. Getting out of tobacco sales becomes a matter of promoting better health, with caring and integrity.

I'm sure that CVS will make that loss of revenue back elsewhere because it will create more credibility with the company's stakeholders—even more so because the company is living to its purpose and to its values.

Normally, in an established business, where no core company values are available, they are not defined; rather, they are identified through a discovery process. In a start-up, since there is no history yet, I suggest starting out with the values of the founder or founders and revisiting them along the way.

Back in 2001, when my company had fewer than 30 employees, we all were "silently" aware of what we valued and pretty much lived by those values. But we did not have them in writing nor did we have formal discussions about them, and that is the case with most start-ups or small businesses.

But then we grew to more than 150 employees by 2006. We hired a lot of people because we had a lot of work. Many of them, as it turned out, did not share the values of the initial group. Today, I attribute much of our 2008 turmoil to our lack of a shared vision, starting with a formal set of shared values.

I have seen many companies with what I call "compliance" or "look good" values, but when you dig deeper you find out that most of the leaders and employees cannot name them and do not live by them. A business must take seriously the need for a set of core values. It's not just for show.

2. THE CORE PURPOSE OF YOUR BUSINESS

In previous chapters, we have thoroughly discussed the importance of purpose. According to Jim Collins, an organization's core purpose is its reason for existing and must answer the question: "What difference are we making in the world?" The definition of the core purpose of your company must go beyond making money or creating jobs.

Ask yourself why your business exists and what difference it makes in the lives of your customers. To succeed in any endeavor, you need that clarity of purpose. For example, my purpose in writing this book is to help you, as an entrepreneur, grow together with your business instead of being outgrown by it. And I do this by directing you to a set of concepts and tools for mastering your life in business. In doing so, I am not inventing anything, but I am arranging the universe of information that is out there into the logical order of the three challenges.

Numerous thought leaders have addressed the need for purpose and clarity to succeed in any endeavor. Here is a sampling:

- Friedrich Nietzsche (1844–1900), German philosopher, wrote: "He who has the *why* to live can bear almost any *how*."

- Napoleon Hill (1983–1970), journalist, author of *Think and Grow Rich* (1937), one of the best-selling books on personal success, defined his term "definiteness of purpose" as "the starting point of all achievement."

- Victor E. Frankl (1905–1997), Austrian psychiatrist, Holocaust survivor, the founder of Logotherapy, and author of *Man's Search for Meaning*, wrote that people in the concentration camps who could see a purpose for living had a far better chance of surviving. He taught his students that success couldn't be pursued; it must ensue as an unintended side effect of one's personal dedication to a cause greater than oneself. Frankl often cited Nietzsche's quote from the previous page.

- Michael E. Gerber introduces the concept of the "personal dream" and the "impersonal dream" in his book *Awakening the Entrepreneur Within*. He says the latter are the dreams that reach out beyond ourselves and that result in transcendent companies, as opposed to the companies that are born out of a "personal dream," which seek only to satisfy the personal aspiration of the owner, which normally is about making money.

- Simon Sinek, author and speaker, explains in his best-selling book *Start With Why* that those who have the answer to this question are better able to attract others to their cause. When organizations are clear about why they exist, they are more likely to inspire their employees and attract customers to their products. He says, "people don't buy what you do, they buy why you do it."

That same concept of purpose and its supreme importance has been advanced by businesspeople themselves:

- In March of 2014, I attended an international conference organized by EO in Cancun, where I was also a speaker. There, some of my peers and I had the privilege of being at a private lunch meeting with John Mackey, founder and co-CEO of Whole Foods Market and coauthor of *Conscious Capitalism*. In his keynote and during the private meeting, he attributed his success mainly to being clear about the purpose, saying, "Great companies have great purposes."

- A survey conducted by Deloitte in early 2014 among adults working for companies with more than 100 employees revealed that companies with a strong sense of purpose were more confident of their growth expectations, instilled greater confidence in their stakeholders, and were more likely to create a "best place to work." So that's going beyond philosophy. That's a serious firm doing a survey with hard numbers that shows the power of purpose.

Many people talk about entrepreneurship today. Incubators are full of ideas. In technology, for example, it seems that everyone wants to create the next killer app. But will all of them transcend? The answer is no. We must remember that the successful ideas will be the ones that serve an absolutely legitimate purpose and deliver a real value.

As we saw when the tech bubble burst, we must generate ideas for more than just the sake of generating ideas. Sometimes people and companies will buy technology just to buy technology, whether or not they need it. In *Good to Great*, Collins says successful companies use technology purposefully to solve real business problems and are not trying to keep up with the latest fad.

It is realistic and totally acceptable for people to have their own personal purposes for starting a company, but the purpose of the business must go beyond their own purposes.

However, there are times when ideas for a new business will arise from the need to solve a personal issue, problem, or frustration. If you personally are experiencing a situation, it is likely that many others are experiencing something similar, and there may not be a viable solution in place yet. Many entrepreneurs have created and grown successful businesses that way. They have done it based on what I call a "transcendent personal purpose," a personal purpose that goes beyond oneself.

A friend in Mexico was looking for a safe environment where his daughters could learn about show business. They wanted to become singers, but show business can be a dangerous world for young people who could face physical and moral abuse. He traveled to Hollywood to learn more about the industry and happened to meet another gentleman from Mexico who eventually became his business partner. They created an academy that teaches kids to sing, act, and perform and that represents them in the industry while keeping a close watch on their integrity. He found a true opportunity and a true purpose based on a personal need.

In the book *Big Data: A Revolution That Will Transform How We Live, Work and Think,* there is a story about Oren Etzioni, a computer scientist, who was angered after finding out that he had paid much more for an airfare than the passenger sitting next to him, even though he had purchased his ticket way in advance. Irritated by the erratic behavior of airline fares, he founded *Farecast,* a travel price prediction site that would tell you if a fare was most likely to go up or go down. The company was sold to Microsoft in 2008 for $110 million dollars. Again: a true need, a true opportunity, and true purpose that was very well rewarded.

As you can see, philosophers, entrepreneurs, and consulting firms have been emphasizing and demonstrating the supreme importance of purpose. In business and in life itself, you need authenticity if you are to thrive. **When you are in the process of defining your company's purpose, it is important**

that you focus on the problem you intend to solve and not on the solution you pretend to sell. If you serve a real need or solve a real problem, your enterprise will have a bigger chance to succeed. Otherwise, it may fade away.

3. PURPOSE, VISION, AND MISSION STATEMENTS

And so, is it the mission and then the vision? Or is it the vision and then the mission? And now, many companies are using purpose statements—and some of them instead of mission statements. For many years with my company, I tried to define the mission of the vision and the vision of the mission, and I was never completely satisfied with the outcomes. When I asked others, they seemed as confused by the question as I was.

I have seen many companies, gathered different opinions, read a lot of literature, and consulted with several experts, just to realize that there is no consensus around how these statements should be used.

The conclusion that I have personally reached and become comfortable with is that vision and mission statements can be used to describe how you are going to fulfill your company's core purpose. From my point of view, the vision statement refers to an ideal for the long-term future, being ten years or more. I like to see the mission statement rather as a mid-term—three to five years—description of where your business needs to be heading, the field where it is going to play (also known as your "sandbox"), and what it is doing in the present moment.

First you define your core purpose, which is about the problem you intend to solve. Then you define your vision, which is an aspirational statement of where you see your company in the long-term. This long-term vision could be ten years or more. And last, your mission; it is what you must do mid-term—in three to five years—to fulfill that purpose and vision.

For example, CVS' company purpose is: "Helping people on their path to better health." I think there may be other ways to fulfill that purpose. It could become a hospital; it could become a research company. There are many ways to help people to have better health, but for now CVS chooses to be a pharmacy. So, from my point of view, that's their current mission.

Collins and Porras, in various works, introduced a powerful concept to build a compelling vision for a company. It is called the Big Hairy Audacious Goal, or BHAG, and I learned about it through the Gazelles materials and in Collins' book, *Good to Great*. A BHAG is an ambitious target with a horizon of ten to 25 years.

The characteristics of a BHAG are that it must be measurable and realistic but ambitious enough to not know how you are going to get there. A BHAG can be quantitative—as in revenue or number of units built or customers served—or it can be qualitative. The objective of a BHAG is to help you connect with your core purpose. As products and fashions change, you need that BHAG to keep in touch with your core purpose.

A BHAG should be vibrant, engaging, tangible, but at the same time should bring some discomfort: How on earth will you get there? The article gives several examples, including these: "Become a $125 billion company by year 2000" (Walmart, 1990) and "Become the Harvard of the West" (Stanford University, 1940s).

At a strategy workshop that I was delivering at the EO Accelerator Program in Mexico, a fellow member who owns a company that does installations for the pharmaceutical industry described their BHAG set in 2012. They are aiming for "300 successful projects by 2022."

If, at the moment we set a BHAG, we know the path to achieve it, it's not ambitious enough to be a BHAG. It is because it is audacious that it helps you focus on the overall vision. You can build your mission from there.

Once you are clear about the core purpose of your company, I suggest that you base your vision statement on your BHAG (10 to 25 years) and your mission statement on what you need to achieve on a three- to five-year outlook. You will have further input for this when we discuss the "One Page Strategic Plan" in the next section.

Remember: (1) Purpose statement, (2) vision statement, and (3) mission statement. That's the order, and I recommend making them as concise and as short as possible.

4. THE STAGE YOUR BUSINESS IS IN

As part of the EO events, I attended a compelling keynote delivered by Arnoldo de la Rocha, the founder of Pollo Feliz, a successful chain of roasted chicken fast food restaurants with more than 700 units all over Mexico as well as in Arizona and Texas.

"The wise man knows how to live according to his age," de la Rocha said, and that resonated with me. Even though his talk was mostly on personal matters, I recognized that this wisdom applied to business as well.

When executives from large corporations decide to become entrepreneurs, they often make the mistake of running their new venture the way they used to run their job. I have seen some of them rent fancy offices. They may even keep flying first class. And what they see is just a faster burn rate of their capital.

Similarly, when companies small or large open a new business unit, they will often try to run it as they do the rest of the company. That has happened to me. When I started my business in 1996, I began small, out of a home office. I took great care with expenses and overhead. But as we grew and started to add business units, I wouldn't follow that golden rule of starting out small, of testing, of keeping the overhead low. That was a big mistake.

In December of 2013, I attended a workshop on business incubators sponsored by the Mexican chapter of the National Business Incubation Association (NBIA). The workshop was held at the incubator unit of a university in Monterrey for student-founded companies. One, however, had been started by a larger company, a software factory located downtown. They wanted to develop and launch some packaged apps. Instead of creating that division within its own offices, the owners chose to do so in the incubator, with a different team and in a different environment.

The company was aware that its main business was not in the same stage as its start-up. They would be very different entities with different teams and salaries. The company did not want the mature business and the incubating business to interfere with each other.

What stage are you in with your business? Are you a start-up, or are you a mature business creating a start-up? Many companies do not consider the difference in approaches, but it is important that all stakeholders understand the company's stage. We need to live and to act according to our age, as Arnoldo de la Rocha expressed so eloquently, "Wise words for life and also for business."

Daniel Marcos is a fellow coach at Gazelles International and is also a friend of mine. It was he who invited me to become a member of the Gazelles association of coaches. He is passionate about the evolution of companies, and in his keynotes he includes a slide titled "From Entrepreneur to Chief Executive Officer," where he discusses the stages of a business from start-up to large company.

"A start-up must first focus on nailing the product," he says. "A small business must focus on sales, to keep the company alive through the chasm. The mid-sized business must focus on industry definition. And the large business, he says, must focus on dominance."

"A start-up should concern itself with developing the right product until it establishes itself as a small business and then turn its attention to scaling up as it becomes increasingly larger. The large business should continuously grow and aim to dominate its industry."

As Steve Blank, serial entrepreneur and coauthor of *The Startup Owner's Manual*, says, "A start-up is *not* a smaller version of a large company."

5. UNDERSTANDING AND BUILDING ALIGNMENT WITH YOUR STAKEHOLDERS

You need to be sure that your stakeholders share your vision and you share theirs. A stakeholder is a person, group of persons, or organization that has a legitimate interest in your business. Without their support, your organization would cease to exist. The internal stakeholders include your leadership and management, and then your employees and the owners of the company. The external stakeholders include your customers, shareholders, suppliers, and creditors—and also society itself and even the government.

Large companies, with their corporate governance programs and social responsibility programs, have to be aware of the stakeholder concept. Small business owners, however, tend not to think about their stakeholders as a whole. It is important that all of them share the vision of the business and nurture those relationships. All too often, however, small business owners neglect to do so.

During the private lunch we had with John Mackey in Cancun, he told us that back when Whole

Foods Market was getting started, a storm flooded their only store. The next day, customers were helping to clean up the store. Suppliers and creditors were softening their terms. These stakeholders didn't want the business to disappear. They believed in it, and they needed it.

That's what happens when the stakeholders share the company's vision and buy into it. It makes a huge difference.

YOUR COMPANY'S STAKEHOLDERS

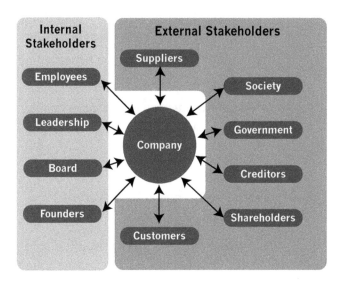

Courtesy of https://commons.wikimedia.org/wiki/
File:Stakeholder_(en).png

I encourage you to make a quick assessment of the stakeholders of your business:

- From 1 to 10, how would you rate the relationship with every stakeholder group? If it is below 10, what would it take to make it a 10?

- From 1 to 10, how would you rate each stakeholder's awareness of your company's vision? If it is below 10, what would it take to make it a 10? In some cases this may not apply. For example, in the case of government, the IRS will care about your taxes, not your vision, so you better be aware of their "vision." But there may be a government agency that is interested in the impact that your business can have in the community.

- From 1 to 10, how relevant is your company for each stakeholder? Again, if the grade is below 10, what would it take to raise it to 10? So take the relevance test. How relevant are you for each of your customers, vendors, employees, and other stakeholders? Would they care if you disappeared?

- From 1 to 10, how aware are you of your stakeholder's needs, vision, etc.?

- Identify your stakeholder's "personas." Find out their needs and interests, how they think, their expectations, and the drivers within their organizations. For example, the large corporations that we have worked with such as Microsoft, SAP, and others normally have what we call a channel manager, or account manager. We have concluded that we must understand how these organizations compensate those managers. If we act in their interest, they will act in ours.

6. YOUR BUSINESS MODEL

Business models are nonetheless essential to mastering a shared vision among stakeholders of a company's direction.

In short, a business model is a representation of how a company generates value and makes money.

A business model has many uses, but among them is its role in helping stakeholders master that shared vision.

The Business Model Canvas

Key Partners	Key Activities	Value Propositions	Customer Relationships	Customer Segments
	Key Resources		Channels	
Cost Structure			Revenue Streams	

Courtesy of Strategyzer (www.strategyzer.com)

The one template that by far has become a standard for documenting business models is the popular Business Model Canvas, initially proposed by Alexander Osterwalder, who with Yves Pigneur wrote *Business Model Generation*, along with 470 practitioners throughout the world.

The Business Model Canvas helps you to think deeply about the nine building blocks for your business, which are:

1)   Your customers

2)   Your value proposition

3)   Your channels

4)   Your customer relationships

5)   Your revenue streams

6)   Your resources

7)   Your activities

8)   Your partnerships

9)   Your cost structure

You can learn more in the book, and I highly recommend it.

The book covers the nine blocks in detail as well as design and assessment techniques of your business model. It also explains five patterns of existing business models based on existing business concepts.

The term "business model patterns" refers to business models with similar characteristics and behaviors. I consider these patterns an extremely important aid in the design of your own business. There is no need to start from scratch, and there is other literature available that discusses a large array of them.

The two day Business Model Generation Workshop, that I attended in San Francisco in November 2013, was a once in a lifetime experience. There were a lot of dynamics on building and assessing existing business models, including the ones for iPod and Nespresso. Steve Blank was a surprise speaker, and my two main takeaways from his talk were: (1) before going big into the market, you should test your business model first, and (2) his widely quoted observation that, "There are no facts inside the building, so get out and talk to customers."

So depending on your company's stage, a business model will be useful. It can either define how your start-up will work, or it can assess whether your established business model is still working effectively. In both cases, it is an invaluable tool to create alignment among stakeholders.

At the start of this chapter, I introduced you to the Disney film *Monsters, Inc.* Today, as a business coach, I have recommended the movie at my workshops and in my keynotes. With childlike clarity, it demonstrates important business principles. The monsters had to reinvent their business model, basing their energy production not on frightening children but on joking with them.

I see that as a great example of the need to reassess your business model. The monsters' value proposition was the same. The purpose of the business was still to generate electricity. The market for that energy hadn't changed. But times had changed. It was time to take a fresh look at how they ran the business.

In section 2, the first lesson that I shared was that **nothing lasts forever**. That includes business models. The monsters realized that nothing lasts forever, even the power of screams. Finally, they realized that they were not in the business of scaring kids, but instead, they were in the business of producing energy. Once they understood their core purpose, the monsters were able to adapt to a new form of energy—laughter—and move forward. In much the same way, I recommend that you assess and revise your business model at least once a year, depending on the nature of your industry.

7. YOUR TARGET CUSTOMER

I hear the same question in all the business development, coaching, consulting, and training programs that I represent or have attended: "Who is your target customer?"

Some of the content is general in nature, and some of it is focused on different stages that a company can be in. They may use varying terminology, but they are addressing the same issue: In *The Start-up Owner's Manual*, Blank proposes the "Customer Development Model"; WKI, a Canadian program for start-ups, simply asks "Who is your customer?"; E-Myth refers to "your most probable customer" and Gazelles to "your core customer." Duct Tape Marketing and Provendus talk about "your ideal customer."

Small companies need to learn how to profile their target customers, which is important at all stages of business. I encourage you to read books or embark on a journey to find the tools that can help you define it. In a nutshell, profiling your customers is about identifying demographic and psychographic characteristics. Demographics in the business-to-consumer environment include gender, location, economic status, etc.; in the business-to-business environment, it's industry, locations, size, and revenue. Psychographics (as *The E-Myth* and *Duct Tape Marketing* explain) refers to why the customer chooses to buy from you, either in a B2C or B2B environment.

Another concept, "buyer persona," goes deeper into customers as human beings. If you are launching a business selling ice cream or juice, you will study how the consumer behaves. But if you work in business-to-business environments, such as I do, you need to look at how people behave within their organizations and how they are motivated, how they are compensated, etc. We sell software used by several people inside the same company. There are several buyer personas—the CEO and the CIO and the CFO, for example. We need to go deeper and truly see the people behind the company profile—their frustrations, their motivations, their holdbacks, and their decision process.

When we launched the E-Myth Mastery Program in Mexico in 2009, we had no history to help us do a profile of our target customer, so we based it on input from E-Myth Worldwide and their experience in the United States, as well as our intuition.

After having gained local experience over a few years, we hired an external coach in 2013 to help us build our buyer persona based on a survey of companies we had coached. We learned interesting information such as age, buying power, academic degree, magazines read, and the reason for engaging, or not engaging, in our program. This has helped us execute more targeted campaigns.

By analyzing the survey, we identified our most successful customers, the ones who followed through with the E-Myth program while obtaining breakthrough results for their businesses. The point is that even in a business-to-business environment, you need to understand the profiles of the people within the company because those are the ones who are buying from you.

When working on your core customer definition, I encourage you also to reflect on the following questions recommended by John Jantsch, creator of the Duct Tape Marketing System and author of several best-selling books:

- What are your customer's expectations?

- How can you meet and exceed these expectations every time? This is also known as your Brand Promise.

- What does it take for your customers to refer you to their friends, clients, and colleagues?

- What makes you unique to your ideal customer? This is also known as your USP (Unique Selling Proposition).

- What kind of customer can you serve best?

- What kind of customer brings out the best of you?

8. YOUR COMPANY'S STORY

In his book *A Whole New Mind*, Daniel Pink says we are moving from the information age to the conceptual age. The era of "left brain" dominance and the Information Age that it engendered is giving way to a new world in which "right brain" qualities such as inventiveness, meaning, and empathy are beginning to predominate.

According to Pink, there are six essential aptitudes, "the six senses," on which professional success and personal satisfaction increasingly will depend: design, story, symphony, empathy, play, and meaning.

I believe people learn more effectively through storytelling. At Gazelles, we use stories of other companies to illustrate the concepts that we teach.

When I deliver my keynotes in workshops, I try to use a lot of stories. That is why I started this book with personal stories and experiences, and I have used anecdotes throughout. I am a natural storyteller, and I have learned to use my right-brain propensities to serve my business best.

One day, about a decade before I became aware of the power of storytelling, I was dealing with a customer who was upset with the software that we were implementing at his company. That happens a lot with enterprise software projects because of the variety of people involved. You inevitably will have sponsors and detractors, too—and I was dealing with one of the latter. The project was stuck.

The more I tried to convince him that they had made the right choice, the harder I was hitting against a wall, until at some point I told him, "You know, I don't like this software because I sell it. I sell the software because I like it. I wish I could tell you the story of how I got into this business."

Even over the telephone, I could sense him breaking into a smile. His attitude quickly changed, and he invited me to have a two-hour Mexican-style lunch (yes, tequila included). I told him my story, and he bought into my passion. Our relationship changed for the better. I even invited him to my next birthday party, and he showed up. From that point, our relationship became smooth, and we managed to finish the project successfully.

In its annual international award competitions for its world partner conference, Microsoft asks applicants to submit the story of their successes. Our company was very good at that: between 2001 and 2010, Fillgap was one of the most awarded partners by Microsoft, to the extent that in her 2006 keynote in front of thousands of attendees, Allison Watson, who was the corporate vice president of the Partner Ecosystem, recognized us as one of three companies in the world deserving special praise.

Three times, Microsoft named us Partner of the Year for Latin America—one time we received an award as the Professional Services Partner of the Year for Latin America, and five times my company was recognized as an Inner Circle Member, among the top 1 percent of partners worldwide.

I put a lot of work into those submissions, as did those who spent hours helping me to edit them. Sometimes I would finish those submissions at three o'clock in the morning. The awards we received were not only because of our great performance—I am certain that our ability to articulate our stories and engage the jury contributed to the honors we received.

You should have a story of what your company does for its customers, including your beliefs, accomplishments, and benefits. You need to share it with your current and prospective stakeholders. Have all your team members be aware of it and share it, too. And when people ask you what your business is about, be prepared to sum it up in one phrase. You should build that phrase based on your purpose statement.

David Kerpen is a social media expert and author of the *Likeable* series of books. When composing a story about your company, I suggest you take two of his recommendations into consideration: (1) be authentic, and (2) be honest and transparent.

Storytelling is powerful. When we share ourselves and we share our stories, we connect with people. I encourage you to use that power with your stakeholders. It is one thing that has worked well for me over and over again, and I am sure it will work well for you too.

MAINTAINING THE SHARED VISION

"You never tell me that you love me," a wife complains to her husband. To which he responds: "Look, of course I love you. I told you so when we got married 30 years ago, and unless I say otherwise, the same condition applies."

That just won't work, you say? Nor will it work in business. Now that you have started to build a shared vision with your stakeholders, the challenge is to maintain it. You need to assess and repeat your vision periodically with all your stakeholders in order to keep it present among all.

In the next chapter we will go deeper into the concept of rhythm and make clear how you can systematically keep your vision alive.

CHALLENGE 3: MASTERING YOUR COMPANY'S PERFORMANCE

Mastering performance is about applying the right balance of strategy, execution, *and* relationships to achieve results. Do you feel overwhelmed by these words? I was too, at one point.

According to the Harvard Business Press, strategy is about understanding what you do, what you want to become and—most importantly—focusing on how you plan to get there.

In the previous chapter, we defined a way to build a shared direction for your business—but there is still work to be done to make the strategy happen. It is known that 85 percent of businesses never execute the plans they create.

In their best-selling book *Execution: The Discipline of Getting Things Done*, Larry Bossidy and Ram Charan present the term "execution" as a systematic process for tenaciously following through and ensuring accountability, which is the missing link between aspirations and results.

Either in the strategic thinking or the execution phase, nurturing your relationships with your stakeholders is critical. You need those skills to keep everyone engaged and motivated in both phases.

APPLYING THE RIGHT BALANCE

Before we discuss the next set of tools, let me share more details of my personal story that will illustrate how I have learned about balancing those three essential ingredients of strategy, execution, and relationships.

Between 2001 and 2006, the revenues of Fillgap grew robustly and consistently year after year. Our strategy was based on having a tight relationship with the software vendors that we represented and remaining closely aligned with them, as well as learning their partner programs in and out and taking advantage of that knowledge. We pursued aggressive marketing, PR, and sales tactics, and we made strategic acquisitions of other companies, in order to have portfolio coverage and a national coverage.

Even though we lacked a systematic execution approach, our tactics for making things happen and following through worked for us then. We did put a lot of focus on sales, not only on our side but with the companies that we acquired. Besides that, we were totally allied with Microsoft, who was our major stakeholder.

In the summer of 2005 at the World Partner Conference (WPC), which Microsoft holds annually for its resellers all over the world, we were presented the Consistent Performance award in front of over 1,000 people. By the summer of 2006, at the next WPC in Boston, our company was the ultimate rock star. This was the conference where Allison Watson, in her keynote in front of 10,000 participants, mentioned me and two others as visionaries and role models. I was enjoying glamorous recognition, receptions, and dinners during the conference, press coverage during the whole event, and I continued to get press coverage for at least a month after I returned from Boston.

Then things began to change. We had grown our offices nationwide. We had more than 150 team members, but we were outgrowing our execution tactics without noticing. Feeling that we were about to make the bigger leagues, I appointed my COO (who had previously been the CFO and who also was a shareholder of the company) as the CEO. One of the first things he suggested was that we merge the offices, which at that time were operating as independent legal entities, into one monolithic company.

It sounded like a great idea, and everybody was excited. The shareholders of the acquired companies also liked the idea. It seemed we would be working more efficiently, but the merger was executed poorly. We did not reorganize well. For one thing, our travel costs skyrocketed. And previously, the shareholders had felt and behaved like entrepreneurs and owners. Now, they were feeling and behaving like employees with stocks. The ways that had worked for the smaller companies did not work for the consolidated operation.

Meanwhile, Microsoft had implemented structural changes to its partner program, and we had not paid sufficient attention to it. Yes, I noticed it, but I did not want to recognize it. The changes had a major impact on our competitive position in the market, on the alignment between Microsoft and us, and also on the alignment between our shareholders.

By the end of 2007, we were starting to lose serious money even though our revenues were still growing. The situation was so bad that my CEO and other managers had to leave, and I had to take over the operation of the company again. By 2008, the operational and cash flow problems were piling up every day. The relationships between all of us started to deteriorate. Then the world financial crisis hit and hit hard. The rest is the story you already know from the beginning of the book.

Today, the social and economic changes that have been taking place during the past years are impacting most industries, including ours. As a result of that, we have become more attentive of the trends, have been restructuring our portfolio, and are exploring new business models.

One of the main things that I have learned from these experiences, as well as from my training and coaching programs, is the importance of applying the right balance of **strategy, execution, and relationships** to our businesses.

As entrepreneurs, we must become experts in balancing these three components. Each business is different, and priorities differ at any given point, and so the recipe may not always be the same. If you apply too much strategic thinking without enough execution, you will stall your business—some call that "paralysis by analysis." If you jump right into execution without having a well thought out strategy, you most likely will wreck your business. If you apply the wrong strategy, you will poison your business even if your execution is impeccable. And remember: **it is essential, as you pursue strategy and execution, to take care of the relationships with your stakeholders.**

To achieve this, there are two particularly valuable tools that I have learned from Gazelles: the "One Page Strategic Plan" and the "meeting rhythms." Both are covered later in this section.

I wish I had been aware about these two tools back in 2001 to 2006 when my company was growing so rapidly. I think we could have saved ourselves a lot of problems, and we most likely would have taken the company to another level.

CONSIDERATIONS AND TOOLS

Let's now take a closer look at what I consider to be the basic considerations and tools to master the performance of your business:

1. Your organization chart and job descriptions

2. Your core processes

3. Mastering your company's finances

4. Conducting a SWOT and a SWT analysis

5. Establishing priorities

6. Your key performance indicators (KPIs)

7. Putting it all together: the One Page Strategic Plan

8. Following through: the meeting rhythm

9. Last but not least: always be marketing and selling

1. YOUR ORGANIZATION CHART AND JOB DESCRIPTIONS

When I first read Gerber's *The E-Myth Revisited* in 2008, I had another "aha" moment as I read the chapter "Your Organizational Strategy."

In that chapter he discusses in an amusing but powerful way how small businesses tend to organize around their people instead of around the tasks to be done. He explains how to create an organization chart and write "position contracts" (which are a proprietary version of regular job descriptions plus further accountability and commitment components). As a standard part of the program, we teach our E-Myth clients how to develop their organization charts and write position contracts for team members.

At the Gazelles workshops (both public and private), we hand out a sheet called the "Function Accountability Chart" that shows standard positions inside a company. We ask participants to fill in the name of the person accountable for each position. We find that different people in the same company, including midsized firms, fill out the chart differently, indicating that an organization chart is not well communicated or does not even exist.

One of our clients told us that after implementing the organizational chart and position contracts, the company not only was more efficient in its inside operations but also dramatically improved its recruitment process. Also, a non-profit organization in Mexico, which I have coached on a pro-bono basis, has been able to make better use of its volunteers after developing its organizational chart and writing the job descriptions.

As you design your organization chart and your job descriptions, consider the following:

- Again, think like an investor. When shareholders work inside the company, it is tempting to design the organization around them and the compensation packages around their needs. It is here where multiple-headed monsters are born. Organizations might have two or more co-CEOs, or they might not even have a CEO so as not to hurt anyone's sensitivities. I have seen large organizations with co-CEOs, such as SAP, Whole Foods Market, and Cinemex, operate successfully with the co-CEO model at some point. But normally there is one person who needs to be in charge and have the last word. Whole Foods' John Mackey told me it takes trust and respect to make the model work.

- Design the organization, job descriptions, accountabilities, *and* the compensations as if you would be hiring from the outside to fill all positions. Only after doing that should you decide which positions can be occupied by shareholders, who need to be open to the possibility of stepping aside if they don't fulfill the defined expectations or if the job outgrows them. As I explained in "Challenge 1: Mastering Yourself First," your business is part of your wealth, and it can also be your job—so you need to separate those aspects if you expect your business to grow beyond yourself. A close friend recently left his position as sales director of his own company, agreeing with his partners that to reach the next level in sales, they needed someone with different skills and experiences. He is still a shareholder of that company and sits on the board; meanwhile, he is looking to build a new business and spending more time with his family. He tells me that these have been some of the most fulfilling times in his life.

- Never, ever, ever have one person report to more than one boss: This is a recipe for disaster. It is okay to have a "combo role" where one person occupies two or more positions, especially in small organizations, but always reporting to *one* person.

- Collins points out that great companies have the right structure with the right people doing the right things right. To do things consistently and to delegate effectively, you need a well-designed organization with a well-established set of values (discussed in the previous chapter) and well-defined processes (discussed next). That's how you attract and retain great talent. You want an environment where people will be happy to work.

- And remember, on top of your organization, there must be a board of directors and/or an advisory board that protects the interests of the company and the shareholders.

2. YOUR CORE PROCESSES

Every organization should have a common set of documented core business processes in order for it to function properly. That's what Collins means by doing the right things right.

Small organizations should start with basic processes in five core areas, test them out, and then grow from there in number and sophistication:

1. Marketing and sales

2. Procurement, production, and inventory

3. Delivery

4. Billing and collections

5. Back office: finance, administration, and human resources

We work with many business owners who say they have no processes inside their organizations. Actually, they do have some processes, since every organization does have its way of doing things—but the issue is that those ways aren't documented. The important thing is to document, optimize, communicate, and implement those processes.

As discussed in section 2, E-Myth has a tool called "The Key Frustration Process," which we use with our clients to help them identify flaws in how they do things. From there, they can make the necessary improvements.

During our Gazelles workshops we use another tool called the "Process Accountability Chart" to create alignment on who is responsible for each process and how they are measured. As in the Function Accountability Chart, we often find that different team members of the company see processes differently.

3. MASTERING YOUR COMPANY'S FINANCES

Accounting is what I consider to be one of the two languages of business (besides English). If you want to own a business, it is imperative that you possess full understanding of how accounting works. This is non-negotiable!

I have been in the business of implementing accounting systems and ERP (Enterprise Resource Planning) systems for midsize companies for more than 20 years. The biggest challenge I tend to see with our customers—including IT staff, executives, and even CEOs—is the lack of accounting knowledge. The best consultants we have are those with accounting degrees or, at least, a deep accounting knowledge.

At our E-Myth practice (where we coach small companies), the main challenge for most business owners is not only the accounting piece but also being aware of their overall finances. This has led us to implement a practice where in every session, our coaches ask our clients specific questions about their finances such as revenues, costs, expenses, profits, cash flow, etc. By implementing this practice, we once helped one of our clients realize that the company was two months away from running out of cash. The client was able to apply the necessary measures.

These are some basic and key financial reports and indicators that every business owner should master:

- **Profit and loss:** Summarizes revenues, costs, and expenses for a specific period and ends with the bottom line profit or loss for that period. A profit and loss statement is like a movie on how a company did financially during a specific time frame.

- **Balance sheet:** Summarizes the financial condition of the company consisting of amounts for assets, liabilities, and owner's equity for a closing date of a specific period. Opposed to the profit and loss statement, a balance sheet is like a photo of the financial situation of the company at a specific date.

- **Cash flow:** Summarizes sources and uses of cash for a specific period, the net cash increase or decrease, and the reasons this figure is different than the bottom line net income or loss (profit and loss statement) for that period.

- **Break-even point, fixed costs, and margin:** Every business has fixed costs, such as payroll, rent, etc. To make a profit, you need to get over your fixed costs by selling with the appropriate profit margin.

- **Budgets and projections:** The purpose of these reports is to plan for the future, compare actual performance, and adjust course of action. You will normally want to project profit and loss as well as cash flow.

- **Financial ratios:** Used to interpret the financial condition of a company based on the figures described above. Most common ratios are: liquidity, working capital, profit ratio, return on capital, and earning per share.

It is the combination of those six that provides a holistic view of the financial performance and situation of your business. A problem that I have seen is when CEOs and business owners operate solely on a cash flow report basis. While cash is king (as it is said), this is dangerous and can lead us to the wrong decisions: a company may be spending cash that does not belong to it without noticing. On the other side, running a business solely on a profit and loss report basis can be just as misleading and dangerous: you see only the profit on paper and may run out of real money to operate the business.

Greg Crabtree, a recognized CPA for growth companies and author of the book *Simple Numbers, Straight Talk, Big Profits!*, says, "When it comes to cash flow, profitability matters the most," meaning that it all starts with profit, but it is not the only thing you need to monitor; you need to monitor the cash too.

Be aware that growing businesses are more cash demanding since you need to acquire more assets, resources, and people to support the higher amount of sales. It is recommended that growth companies have at least six months of cash available to fund their operations.

On the other hand, when you are running an early stage start-up, as opposed to an established company, the most important metric will not necessarily be the profitability of the business but the "burn rate," which is the pace at which you are spending your funds to build the business. Again, as discussed previously, be aware of the stage your company is in and run it accordingly.

4. CONDUCTING A SWOT AND A SWT ANALYSIS

The SWOT analysis is a traditional strategic planning tool that will allow you to evaluate your company's strengths, weaknesses, opportunities, and threats.

SWOT Analysis

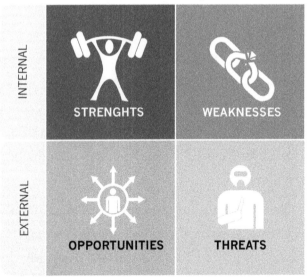

You will need to identify these elements by conducting discussions with your team and perhaps other stakeholders. As you identify them, you will distribute these four elements into a matrix where the "strengths" and "weaknesses" are internal to your organization, as opposed to the "opportunities" and "threats" that are external.

SWT Analysis

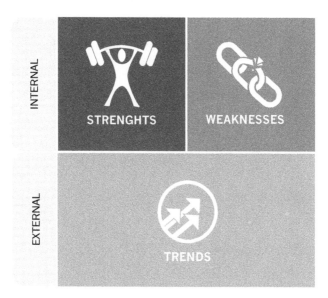

Courtesy of Gazelles

The SWT analysis is an augmented version of the original SWOT and was introduced by Gazelles to have a more strategic view. The SWOT is not to be replaced by the SWT; the first one is meant for the middle management, while the latter is meant for the senior management and the board. If your company is still small, you will most likely be wearing middle and senior management hats and will need to be involved in both.

The big difference that you will notice in the SWT is that the "opportunities" and "threats" have been replaced by "trends." When we talk about trends, we are referring to topics such as major changes in technology, your industry, social and consumer behaviors, business models, competitive landscape, economic and political developments, etc.

Developing a SWT analysis and becoming aware of the trends that can affect your business will help you deal in a systematic way with the fact that **nothing lasts forever,** which we discussed in the first lesson of section 2.

Being aware of your SWOT and your SWT and defining how to work on the items that you discovered will be the starting point to define initiatives and establish priorities, which are discussed next.

5. ESTABLISHING PRIORITIES

There will always be many things that you need or want to do in your company. The key here is to identify a handful of possible activities that will have the biggest impact in a specific period. Normally there are between three and five but not more.

But how do we make sure that we establish the right priorities? Just as we previously discussed on how to set personal priorities, I recommend that you use the same thinking process to become clear about what your company needs to focus on:

1) Which item could you work on, even if it takes a big effort and a considerable amount of time and resources, so that by implementing it, it would have the biggest impact in your business? This could be something that could bring you closer to your vision, or it could be resolving a big issue that is keeping you from advancing toward your vision.

2) On which item could you apply some easy-to-implement activities that could have a big short-term benefit that would

either help or motivate you and your team to get the larger items done?

Once you have set your company's priorities, you will need to share them with your team and get everyone on board in order to accomplish them. When everyone on the team is in agreement and working together on the same priorities, you get alignment.

6. YOUR KEY PERFORMANCE INDICATORS

"Things that get measured get done" is a phrase that I learned from Jack Daly, expert in sales management and author of *Hyper Sales Growth*.

You cannot manage what you do not measure, so in order to assess your progress you need to be able to measure it against a specific goal or target.

The purpose of Key Performance Indicators (KPIs) in a business is to evaluate the success of the organization as whole, as well as a particular area or position, process, or goal, measured against established targets that may or may not be financial. The targets are based on key elements needed to fulfill the business strategy.

Examples of financial KPIs in a company are gross revenue, gross profit margin, net profit margin, return on investment (ROI), etc.

Examples of nonfinancial KPIs are customer satisfaction, market share, capacity utilization, quality index, employee satisfaction, brand positioning, etc.

External stakeholders also play an important part in how KPIs are established. For example, software companies evaluate their resellers not only on sales quota but also on year-over-year growth, customer additions, customer satisfaction, customer retention, and number of certified consultants.

When you start establishing your KPIs, be careful to not implement too many at once. The same as with core processes: start basic, test out, and grow in quantity and sophistication over time.

7. PUTTING IT ALL TOGETHER: THE ONE PAGE STRATEGIC PLAN (OPSP)

The purpose of the OPSP is to assist you in building your company's vision so your team and other stakeholders can align around it. As its name says, it will help you put your strategic plan together in one single action-oriented page. The use of this powerful tool is absolutely critical to outline your strategy and the way you then proceed to execute it. Most of the components to build your first draft are the ones that we have been discussing throughout this book.

The OPSP was first introduced by Gazelles in the early 2000s; today more than 40,000 companies worldwide are using it, and the number keeps growing.

I am providing you here with a brief description of the OPSP and its benefits. However, to get completely familiarized with it and learn how it works, you need to go directly to the source, the book *Scaling Up* by Verne Harnish.

This tool will help you apply the right balance of strategy, execution, and relationships as you go through a structured thought process involving all these elements in your business.

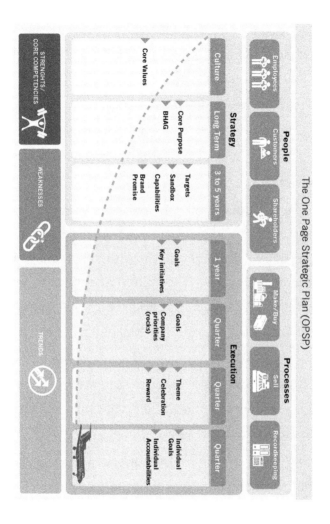

The One Page Strategic Plan (OPSP)

So let me to briefly go over it:

On the top, the one-page plan will help you balance people (reputation drivers) and processes (productivity drivers) by defining the corresponding KPIs for monitoring each of them.

On the bottom, you will find space for your SWT analysis (strengths, weaknesses, and trends), which we discussed earlier.

And in the middle, the OPSP has seven columns that lead you all the way from long-term strategic thinking to individual quarterly accountabilities of your team.

The first three columns are about strategy: they focus on items like your values, your purpose, and your BHAG, down to your three- to five-year targets, including what capabilities you must develop to get there and your sandbox (the field where your company is going to play).

The last four columns are about execution: They focus on things like your yearly and quarterly priorities, your quarterly theme, and individual accountabilities for each area of your company.

As Verne says, the OPSP is not necessarily for public consumption. It is meant instead to help the team get the technical aspects of the strategic plan correct. Once the plan is built, it will be easier and faster to build the messages that communicate the vision to employees and other stakeholders.

8. FOLLOWING THROUGH: THE MEETING RHYTHM

The other invaluable tool that I mentioned early in this chapter is the meeting rhythm, which will help a business to follow up on a plan, apply the necessary changes, and resolve issues as they arise.

Yes, I know, most of us hate meetings and would like fewer meetings instead of more. However, what I have learned over the years and with the help of these tools, is that the problem is not in the meetings themselves but in their purpose, agenda, content, and duration.

To get the most value out of meetings, Gazelles proposes five types of them, arranged in a yearly, quarterly, monthly, weekly, and daily rhythm:

	Purpose	Persons Involved	Duration
Annual	•Define and revisit strategy, mid-term targets, and goals for the year. •Review old plan. •Check current reality. •Develop new plan.	•Leadership and management •Update to all the company when plan is finished	An average of two to three days each year
Quarterly	•Review quarter and set priorities and goals for the next three months	Same as annual	An average of one day or less
Monthly	•Monthly review •Lessons learned	Frontline, middle and upper management/ leadership	Half a day to a full day
Weekly	•Status update •Operational/ tactical	All the team	An average of 90 minutes
Daily Huddle	•Daily synchronization at all levels •To expose issues, not resolve them on the spot	All the team	An average of 7 to 15 minutes

Iván Gutiérrez, a very successful entrepreneur and executive in Mexico, has turned three companies around and is now the CEO of Central, the nation's largest parking garage company. He not only applied the OPSP, but he also developed a whiteboard based on it with the most important KPIs for everybody in the company to see.

They run a daily huddle, gathering all the employees at their corporate offices in the large conference room where the whiteboard is. The meeting is the first activity of the day, lasting about 30 minutes, and the main benefit according to Ivan is that he can understand the daily status of his company in a half hour instead of several hours. He has also created a common language in the company through which people can express themselves.

A whiteboard, such as the one used at Central, is a good idea. It can communicate both the OPSP and the established meeting rhythm. Besides that, there is also a software solution to create the OPSP and manage KPIs and the meeting rhythms. It is called Align—it is provided by Gazelles International and is available through our network of coaches.

In addition to the types of meetings discussed, as Gazelles coaches we also recommend establishing a "council" in addition to the weekly management meeting. The purpose of this council is to discuss strategies and the bigger opportunities and challenges facing the company. A few key leaders should form this council, and it is not to be confused with the advisory board or the board of directors.

9. LAST BUT NOT LEAST: ALWAYS BE MARKETING AND SELLING

In December of 2009, I attended a training program for public speakers in Los Angeles led by James Malinchak, an authority in this field. One of his key messages for success was "ABM: Always Be Marketing." Inspired on that phrase, I have added "and Selling" to it.

In 1998, during the early stages of my company, I presented our business plan to Bernardo de la Cabada, who was the managing director of Solomon Software Mexico at that time and is now a good friend of mine. His immediate question was: "Who is going to sell?" We were lacking a strong enough sales team, and he noticed that immediately, so I took his feedback to heart and equipped the company with a marketing, sales, and presales team and spent a lot of time in sales myself. Our company rapidly became one of the top resellers for Solomon, not only in Mexico but also in Latin America. Solomon was acquired by its competitor, Great Plains, in 2000, and in 2001, Microsoft acquired Great Plains. So we became a Microsoft Business Solutions reseller. Following this practice, we became their top reseller in Latin America from 2003 to 2006, four years in a row.

In 2010, I told a friend who serves as a board member in several companies that I was leaving my CEO position and only was going to remain as the chairman. His suggestion was "if you want to add the most value to the company, become a selling chairman." So I did, and as I explained before, through my networking activities I managed to land 30 percent of the contracts the company signed that year.

At our 2011 planning meeting, when the managing director for one of our business units presented a plan that, from my point of view, was too much focused on operations and management, I asked him the same question I was asked by my friend Bernardo 13 years earlier: "Who is going to sell?" We took action, and I convinced him to leave the operations part to our CEO and focus only on sales. Our 2011 revenues and profits for that business unit grew substantially over 2010.

In 2012 we hired a sales director out of a large software corporation, and our focus as owners gravitated toward other "important things." The results were a disaster.

During the past years, E-Myth Worldwide has conducted a yearly survey called "State of the Business Owner" (SOBO). One of the findings in 2014 was that the most successful entrepreneurs were spending at least 40 percent of their time in revenue-generating activities. Their recommendation: "Spend at least two days a week in marketing and sales, even if you think you are too busy."

Many people have told me that they are not good in sales, when the truth is that they do a tremendous job engaging their prospects once they are put in front of them. These persons may not be good at generating leads or closing the sale or either one, but with the right approach, they can learn those skills or surround themselves with other people that do possess those skills. Many years ago I pulled our technical support manager out of her area and put her in sales because some of us saw a potential in her. At the beginning she was terrified, but she did learn the skills that were missing and turned out to be a top performer for us and a top salesperson inside the Microsoft channel. Today she is the sales director for a multinational IT company with offices in Mexico and is responsible for the sales of that company in the Latin American region.

I have learned that the function of marketing and sales must be set up with a systematic approach. Marketing begins with understanding the ideal customer and the market (size, competition, etc.) for your value proposition and generating qualified leads "that know, like and trust you." Selling is about converting those leads into customers who give you repeat business and referrals. To build your own marketing and sales process based on these considerations, begin by becoming familiar with the system presented in *Duct Tape Marketing* by John Jantsch.

FINAL THOUGHTS

IT ALL STARTS WITH YOU

So what does a successful path in your life as an entrepreneur really look like?

The book *StrengthsFinder* authored by Tom Rath and published by Gallup is a great resource for becoming aware of what you do best and how to build upon it. It will guide you through how to identify your top five strengths. The book suggests that building on those strengths will bring you a greater return on investment than trying to fix your weaknesses—and that makes perfect sense to me.

The online assessment included with the book revealed my five strengths: I turned out to be a strategic, a futurist, a positive, an input, and an adaptable person.

In discussing this with a coach, she gave me some homework. "Let's write down some things in two columns," she said. "First, how can you leverage those strengths? And second, how might those strengths also represent a weakness that holds you back?" A strength comes with an inherent weakness. If you do not pay attention to that inherent weakness, it can neutralize your strength and prevent you from growing.

I have learned that becoming aware of an inherent weakness will help to build on a strength because we allow ourselves to learn, acquire useful habits, and overcome limiting beliefs.

You may already be finding yourself experiencing greater success. Does that mean you are done? If you've found success, you may think that you have already mastered these three challenges, that you are at the top, and that you have made it. However, I have learned the hard way that finding success in your business life and mastering the three challenges is NOT like climbing a pyramid. Some of the traits that made you successful at the beginning can act as inhibitors for continued success.

THE WRONG WAY TO SEE
THE THREE CHALLENGES

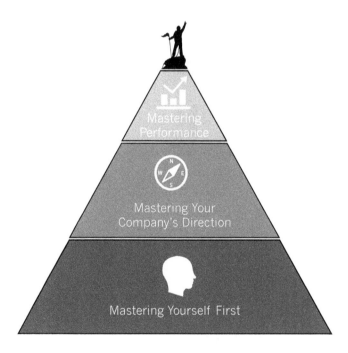

A successful path in your business life favors a never-ending circle. If you are successful, you need to start all over again. Master yourself, master the direction, and master the performance.

THE THREE CHALLENGES MODEL

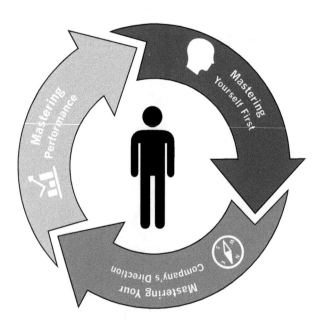

Why? Because if you ever stop growing as a person, you will stagnate. And if you stagnate, you will start to go backward. The pyramid illustration doesn't reflect the fact that when you reach the top, you are really only at the bottom of another, greater pyramid, reaching ever higher. Once again you need to master yourself and the direction and the performance. Once again you need to grow. I believe that you can grow as far and as long and as high as your aspirations, your skills, and your focused actions take you. And I am not necessarily talking about financial growth; there are many ways that you can choose to grow.

As I was about to finish this work, I realized that I was addressing a large part of it to my past self. I had been telling that younger man what he needed to understand about life as an entrepreneur. And now, as I have been sharing the things with you that I wish I had known then, I have also been telling my present self what I need to remember.

I hope that you benefit from reading this book as much as I have benefited from writing it. And I also hope that it has opened your eyes, expanded your awareness, and motivated you to go deeper into the concepts and tools presented here. May they serve you well in your business and in your life.

Keep on growing personally and professionally—because, when it comes to life in business, it all starts with you.

RESOURCES

RECOMMENDED READING

The ideas I gathered from the books listed below are the ones that have had the biggest impact on the way I see life and business. Many of these books are page-turners that I have read cover to cover, and others I have consulted for reference.

I offer you this list as an additional resource; you may have read some or many of them too, but I think it is always good to have a reminder. I have arranged them by topic and in alphabetical order. Enjoy!

PERSONAL

- *Eat That Frog: 21 Great Ways to Stop Procrastinating and Get More Done in Less Time*, Brian Tracy

- *Flow: The Psychology of Happiness*, Mihaly Csíkszentmihályi

- *Having It All: Achieving Your Life's Goals and Dreams*, John Assaraf

- *Rich Dad's Cash Flow Quadrant: Guide to Financial Freedom*, Robert Kiyosaki

- *The Success Principles: How to Get from Where You Are to Where you Want to Be*, Jack Canfield

- *Think and Grow Rich*, Napoleon Hill

- *StrengthsFinder 2.0*, Tom Rath

- *What Got You Here Won't Get You There: How Successful People Become Even More Successful*, Marshall Goldsmith

LEADERSHIP

- *The 21 Irrefutable Laws of Leadership: Follow Them and People Will Follow You,* John Maxwell

- *The Five Dysfunctions of a Team: A Leadership Fable,* Patrick Lencioni

BUSINESS

- *Building Your Company's Vision (Harvard Business Review article),* Jim Collins and Jerry Porras

- *Business Model Generation: A Handbook for Visionaries, Game Changers, and Challengers,* Alexander Osterwalder and Yves Pigneur

- *Duct Tape Marketing: The World's Most Practical Small Business Marketing Guide,* John Jantsch

- *Good to Great: Why Some Companies Make the Leap… And Others Don't,* Jim Collins and Jerry Porras

- *Key Performance Indicators for Dummies (and all his other books on KPIs)*, Bernard Marr

- *Scaling Up: How a Few Companies Make It… and Why the Rest Don't*, Verne Harnish

- *The E-Myth Revisited: Why Most Small Businesses Don't Work and What to Do About It*, Michael E. Gerber

- *The Lean Startup: How Today's Entrepreneurs Use Continuous Innovation to Create Radically Successful Businesses*, Eric Ries

- *The Pumpkin Plan: A Simple Strategy to Grow a Remarkable Business in Any Field*, Mike Michalowicz

- *Simple Numbers, Straight Talk, Big Profits!: 4 Keys to Unlock Your Business Potential*, Greg Crabtree

INSPIRATIONAL

- *Awakening the Entrepreneur Within: How Ordinary People Can Create Extraordinary Companies,* Michael E. Gerber

- *Conversations with God: An Uncommon Dialogue,* Neale Donald Walsh

- *The Alchemist,* Paulo Coelho

- *The Dip: A Little Book That Teaches You When to Quit (and When to Stick),* Seth Godin

- *Te Desafío a Prosperar (I Dare You to Prosper),* Carlos Cuauhtemoc Sánchez (You will need to know Spanish and a bit of the Latin American culture to fully understand this book.)

For continued recommendations on books and articles, please visit www.TheThreeChallenges.com

OTHER RESOURCES

MOVIES

- *Monsters, Inc.*—On business model innovation.

- *Monsters University*—On understanding how people with different strengths can achieve outstanding results when they team up.

- *The Secret*—On applying the law of attraction to fulfill your potential and achieve great results.

Please visit
www.TheThreeChallenges.com
for reviews, downloads, and links to other sites.

ACKNOWLEDGEMENTS

In this section, I would like to acknowledge and wholeheartedly thank all the people who, in some way, contributed to the making of this book.

Some participated directly, several experts and thought leaders have influenced the way I see life and business, and other persons gave me valuable feedback and coaching, or simply, their unconditional support. And many more inspired me with ideas, most of them probably without even being aware of it.

THE COMPLETE TEAM AT ADVANTAGE MEDIA GROUP

Adam Witty, Patti Boysen, and especially Bob Sheasley, Scott Neville, Nate Best, Megan Elger, and George Stevens, for working on the front line with me on bringing this book to life.

THE EXPERTS AND THOUGHT LEADERS WHO HAVE INFLUENCED AND CONTINUE TO INFLUENCE MY VISION EVERY DAY

Jack Canfield, Greg Crabtree, Keith Cupp, Ed DeCosta, Michael Gerber, Ridgely Goldsborough, Fern Gorin, Verne Harnish, John Jantsch, Patrick Lencioni, Daniel Marcos, Bernard Marr, Paul Martinelli, John Maxwell, Mike Michalowicz, Alexander Osterwalder, Carlos Cuauhtémoc Sanchez, and many others.

MY CURRENT AND PAST BUSINESS RELATIONSHIPS (INCLUDING

PARTNERS, KEY TEAM MEMBERS, CLIENTS AND CUSTOMERS)

With a special mention to my partners Pablo Hernandez O Hagan, Rodrigo Laddaga, and Edrei Lozano, who I share the mission with of coaching other entrepreneurs in Mexico and Latin America to grow their businesses.

FROM THE TRAINING AND COACHING PROFESSION

Andy Bailey, Felipe del Rio, Juan Folch, Juan Gonzalez, Lluis Gras, Larry Heiman, Ron Huntington, Diana Long, Paulina López, Rony Zagursky, and many other great colleagues from around the world who I know from the different communities I belong to.

MY PEERS AND FRIENDS FROM THE ENTREPRENEURS' ORGANIZATION (EO)

Claudio Bezanilla, Juan Carlos Cante, Juan Pablo Castillo, Jesús (Chui) de la Garza, Luis Espinosa, Luis G. Aspuru, Modesto Gutiérrrez, Alnoor Kassam, Isaac Lekach, Benjamin Mares, Arturo Merino, Heberto

Taracena, Viviana Vargas, and the many other great members from around the world who continuously contribute to EO's collective intelligence.

MY SPECIAL FRIENDS AND ACQUAINTANCES FROM DIFFERENT WALKS OF LIFE

Alfredo Aboumrad, Rafael Becerril, Jered Cady, Ernesto Cordera, Alejandra de la Cruz, Alfredo Melnik, Salvador Villaseñor, and the many other friends and acquaintances who I am grateful for.

MY FAMILY AND LOVED ONES

I treasure the quality conversations I have had with each one of you and that have been invaluable for the conception of this book, especially my nephews Alexander and Christopher.

Corina, from the bottom of my heart, I thank you for your ongoing support and encouragement, and for being in my life.

www.ingramcontent.com/pod-product-compliance
Lightning Source LLC
Jackson TN
JSHW011936131224
75386JS00041B/1405